D0050517

"I sometimes worry that daily devotional books, while being strong on devotion, give up something in terms of theology. It does not need to be this way, and David Mathis, in this Advent devotional, proves that true devotion arises out of theologically rich truth. We are to 'grow in the grace and knowledge of our Lord and Savior Jesus Christ'—I think this excellent little book helps us to do just that."

**MARK JONES**, Pastor, Faith Vancouver PCA;
Author, *Knowing Christ*

"Christmas is a time in which we tend to find joy in traditions. But traditions are not static, and we benefit from sometimes examining and updating them. Perhaps it is time to update your personal or family traditions with this wonderful series of Advent devotionals. They are fresh, applicable, and deeply biblical. They may just become a precious part of your Christmas tradition this year and in the years to come."

**TIM CHALLIES**, Blogger; Author

"No Advent calendars for sale this Christmas can offer what lies behind the windows David Mathis opens in *The Christmas We Didn't Expect*. True to its title, it is full of surprises. So, buy it, and carefully unwrap each Advent treat (no more than one a day, or you may spoil your appetite). Then let it melt slowly on your spiritual taste buds and enjoy what Isaiah (the Christmas prophet) called 'rich food'!"

**SINCLAIR FERGUSON**, Author; Ligonier Teaching Fellow

"For many, the familiar surfaces of the Christmas story cover unexamined depths. Within this warmly devotional and richly theological book, David Mathis meditates upon some of the great truths of the season, exploring wonderful mysteries that will encourage readers to hear its two-thousand-year-old story once again, as if for the first time."

**ALASTAIR ROBERTS**, Author, *Echoes of Exodus*

"While the people, places and plot line of that first Christmas will ring familiar, there are surprising realities surrounding the birth, life, and death of our Savior Jesus that will make your heart sing. With accessible and pastoral prose, Mathis weaves together biblical, doctrinal, and practical truths into a beautiful tapestry that not only introduces us to the many important truths surrounding Jesus' person and work but also reveals why they are so vital to our daily walk with God."

**JULIUS J. KIM**, President, The Gospel Coalition; Visiting Professor of Practical Theology, Westminster Seminary California

"Theologically rich. Heartwarmingly profound. David Mathis is a sure guide to both the simplicity and the complexity of Christ's coming, and he leads us in a way which is deeply thoughtful, refreshingly insightful and thoroughly worshipful. This daily devotional manages to be soaring and searing at the same time. It will cause you to marvel at the Lord Jesus Christ and to think long and hard about what (and how) we're celebrating, and it will breathe new life into the Christmas season. I look forward to using it and pray that others will do the same."

**GARY MILLAR**, Principal, Queensland Theological College

"Christmas contains so many delightful surprises, whether presents tucked secretly under the tree or much-loved visitors arriving at your door with arms full of gifts. These delights pale in comparison, though, to the astounding surprises you'll discover in *The Christmas We Didn't Expect*. David Mathis reveals fascinating twists and turns on every page of the Christmas story. There is always something new to learn about Christ's birth, and this fresh collection of insights truly delivers. My husband, Ken, and I are already planning to use this remarkable book for our devotional reading this Christmas—and we urge you to join us!"

**JONI EARECKSON TADA**, Joni and Friends International Disability Center

*To Gloria*

The Christmas We Didn't Expect
© David C. Mathis 2020

Published by:
The Good Book Company

thegoodbook.com | thegoodbook.co.uk
thegoodbook.com.au | thegoodbook.co.nz | thegoodbook.co.in

ISBN: 9781784984762 | Printed in Denmark

Design by André Parker

# CONTENTS

# A SEASON OF WAITING

Advent is a season of waiting. Children know well how long the wait for Christmas can be, but modern adults are prone to find our lives moving all too fast. Yet Advent is an ancient invitation to slow down. To mark the days and make them count. To relearn a pace of life that is more unhurried and more human. To not let the 24 hours of Christmas Day catch us off guard and unprepared. And to wait for Christmas with patience and hope.

The English word "advent" is from the Latin *adventus*, meaning "arrival" or "coming." The advent primarily in view each December is the first coming of Jesus, now two millennia ago, and as we look back we are reminded as well of his promise to return.

## OPPORTUNITY, NOT OBLIGATION

To be clear, God has not mandated that we celebrate Advent. Or Christmas. Or Easter. Or any other particular feasts and festivals, in contrast to believers in the Old Testament (Exodus 23:14-17; 34:18-23). For early Christians, especially those raised in the Jewish faith, the surprising newness of the new-covenant age was important to learn and reinforce. This is because, under pressure from fellow Jews, young Christians were observing old-covenant festivals as obligatory, and therefore in a way that undermined the exclusive sufficiency of Christ. They needed to be told, "Let no one pass judgment on you in questions of food and drink, or with regard to a festival or a new moon or a Sabbath. These are a shadow of the things to come, but the substance belongs to Christ" (Colossians 2:16-17).

Few of us today may struggle consciously with the same religious pressure that these early Christians felt. But the apostolic warnings remain important. Observing Advent, or any other calendar season or date, does not secure or keep us in God's favor. Christ has finished that work, and, through his Spirit, we are joined to him, receiving the Father's full acceptance by faith alone.

## THIS BOOK

My prayer, then, is that this collection of daily meditations might help you and your kin keep Jesus as the central and greatest treasure of the Advent season and the Christmas that follows. In particular, in the pages ahead, I want to rehearse the surprising twists and stunning turns of God himself being born as man. In this season of waiting—as we wait with *expectant* hope—I want to highlight how much of that first Christmas teemed with the *unexpected*. From the way Jesus came, to who he really is, to the details of his arrival, the first visitors, and then the life that would follow, and how we are called to respond—it was all so unexpected. Over and over again at Christmas, God shows us the distance between the depths of his wisdom and the shallowness of our human expectations.

So I invite you to join me for this Advent. If you're picking this up before December 1, there's an introduction to read perhaps on November 30 or before, or anytime during the month. Then one reading each day, December 1-24, will aim to turn our gaze to Christ and ready our hearts for the feast to come.

**David Mathis**
Minneapolis, Minnesota

# INTRODUCTION

# GOD CAME DOWN

*You shall call his name Jesus, for he will save his people from their sins.*

*Matthew 1:21*

The allure of Christmas has a strange power, even for the unbelieving and seemingly secularized. The season has a kind of draw—a type of "spirit" or "magic"—that makes the winter-solstice festival every bit as big today, in an increasingly post-Christian society, as it was generations ago.

Why does Christmas still have this magnetism in a society that has tried to empty it of its true meaning? The real magic of Christmas is not in gifts and goodies, new toys and familiar traditions, indoor coziness and outdoor snow. What lies at the heart of Christmas, and whispers even to souls seeking to "suppress the truth" (Romans 1:18), is the most stunning and significant fact in the history of the world: *that God himself became one of us.*

The God who created our world, and humanity as

the apex of his creation, came into our world as human not just for show but for our salvation.

Christmas is supernatural. And our secular society is starving deep down for something beyond the natural, rarely admitting it, and not really knowing why. Christmas taps into something hidden in the human soul and woos us, even when it's inconsistent with a mind that professes unbelief.

## HE CAME FROM HEAVEN

For those of us who do gladly confess the Christ of Christmas—as our Lord, Savior, and greatest treasure—we know why Christmas is indeed enchanted; because at the very heart is the essence of the supernatural: God himself entering into our realm. At Christmas God "came down," not just to observe human sin and inflict righteous judgment from the outside (Genesis 11:5) but to be human and work his mercy from within.

The glory of Christmas is not that it marks the birth of some great religious leader but that it celebrates the long-anticipated coming of God himself—the arrival which God wired our souls from the beginning to ache for. "Then shall all the trees of the forest sing for joy before the Lord, for he comes" (Psalm 96:12-13). "Bethlehem … from you shall come forth for me one who is to be ruler in Israel, whose coming forth is from of old, from ancient days" (Micah 5:2).

What God so stunningly reveals at that first Noël is that when he himself finally does come, it is not in cloud or wind or fire or earthquake, or even simply in a still, small voice (1 Kings 19:11-12). But he comes in the fullness of his creation: as human. He comes as one of us and dignifies our own species in doing so. He comes not as a bird of the air, beast of the field, or great sea creature. Christmas marks his "being born in the likeness of men"—the very God who made man, and has long endured our sin with great patience, is now scandalously "found in human form" (Philippians 2:7-8).

## HE CAME AS A SERVANT

It is wonder enough that he came down at all. But when he did, he came not in human glory and comfort and prestige but "emptied himself, by taking the form of a servant" (Philippians 2:7). He came not only as a creature but in poverty, in weakness, in humility.

For a brief moment, on the hill of his transfiguration, three of his disciples caught a glimpse of the divine-human glory for which he was destined. "He was transfigured before them, and his face shone like the sun, and his clothes became white as light" (Matthew 17:2). But the Jesus they knew, day in and day out, on the roads of backwater Galilee, was no dignitary. "Foxes have holes, and birds of the air have nests, but the Son of Man has nowhere to lay his head" (Luke 9:58). His disciples learned firsthand that "even the Son of Man came not to be served but to serve" (Mark 10:45).

## ALL THE WAY TO DEATH

Such service extended, and deepened, far beyond the mere inconveniences of life into costly self-sacrifice—

even the final sacrifice. He came not just to serve but "to give his life as a ransom for many" (Mark 10:45).

It was one thing to wash his men's feet in the upper room. It was another thing to rise from supper, lead them out to the garden, wait in agony for his captors, and walk alone the literally excruciating path that foot-washing anticipated: "He humbled himself by becoming obedient to the point of death, even death on a cross" (Philippians 2:8).

## TO RESCUE HIS PEOPLE

But this was no mere descent from heaven, even to death. This was descent for a purpose. This was humility on mission. The death that God himself came to die was no accident of history. He came to die and live again. The extent of his people's rebellion was matched, and surpassed, only by the extent of his final sacrifice. And in offering that sacrifice he showed us the very heart of love—his own and his Father's. "God shows his love for us in that while we were still sinners, Christ died for us" (Romans 5:8).

The "magic" of Christmas is not just that God himself came from heaven as man. And it is not just that he humbled himself as a servant to meet the needs of others. And it's not even just that he came to die: to unfold his service all the way to death. The magic is that he came down, and did all that, to rescue us. Such was the promise of God's messenger at the time of announcing Jesus' birth: "You shall call his name Jesus, for he will save his people from their sins" (Matthew 1:21).

He came down to rescue us from sin and restore us to the ultimate joy for which we were made: to know and enjoy him. He came to reconcile us "to himself" (Colossians 1:20). He came not to supply us with the bells and whistles of a commercial Christmas, but he "suffered once for sins, the righteous for the unrighteous, *that he might bring us to God*" (1 Peter 3:18).

*Father in heaven, this Advent seal deep within our souls the meaning of this coming. Jesus came not to entertain. He came not merely to make the greatest story. He came to restore us rebels to our God. Advent is personal. Draw us closer in these days ahead to the heart of Christ, which is your own heart, and make his first advent in all its realness and substance more real in the lives we live. In Jesus' name we pray. Amen.*

# An Unexpected Birth

# 1. A CHRISTMAS CAROL
# FOR THE WEAK

*My soul magnifies the Lord,*
*and my spirit rejoices in God my Savior.*

*Luke 1:46-47*

For too long, I misunderstood Mary's Christmas song in Luke 1:46-55 as if it were a journal entry from a peasant girl. After all, I thought, Mary must have understood so little at this point, right?

An angel had told her that she would bear God's long-awaited king (Luke 1:32-33), and that her relative Elizabeth also had miraculously conceived (Luke 1:36). Mary is stunned, no doubt, at these unexpected graces and goes with haste to visit her relative (Luke 1:39), and yet she still seems to know so little when she offers her song of praise.

However, the Gospel writer, Luke, does not treat Mary's poetic words as a mere aside. They are the high point of his first chapter. As the rest of his Gospel makes plain, Luke stewarded what tight space he had with great care, not as an unbiased reporter but as an inspired spokesman for the risen Christ. And while Mary's "Magnificat," as the church has come to call her song (based on its first word in Latin), may sound strange to us today compared with other carols, her lyrics represent some of the most important Christmas lines ever penned.

They give us one of the most profound glimpses into the heart of God in all the Scriptures. (Perhaps you might want to pause and read Luke 1:46-55 before going any further.)

## MARY'S MAGNIFICENT SONG

The song has three distinct parts. The opening lines (v 46-47) declare what Mary is doing in the hymn: praising God. Then (v 48-49) she explains why: because of what God has done for her. Finally, the bulk of her song (v 49-55) marvels at the *surprising* glory of her God, significant not only to her at that first Christmas but to all his people, all the time.

That final section (v 49-55), which is remarkably God-centered (he is the subject of every verb), is the heart of Mary's hymn and is a celebration of God and his ways, which are so counter to our natural human expectations. Mary celebrates the kind of God he is: different than our instincts and shattering our paradigms as he shows his strength not by recruiting the strong but by rescuing the weak.

When Mary gives the reason for her praise (v 48-49), it is curiously general. As such it follows the pattern of the Psalms. This is emphatically not a personal journal entry, but a song designed for the people of God, in all places, for generations to come.

## GOD'S SURPRISING GLORY

Here, as a skilled theologian—or simply as one well-steeped in the Scriptures (compare Hannah's song in 1 Samuel 2)—Mary holds up the heart of God's holiness ("holy is his name," Luke 1:49): that he is, in himself, of an order altogether different and greater than his creatures. He consistently acts contrary to our human intuitions. His thoughts are not our thoughts, nor his ways our ways, but they are higher—as high as the heavens are above the earth (Isaiah 55:8-9). This God rallies to the weak, not the strong.

He chooses what is foolish in the world to shame the wise. He chooses what is weak in the world to shame the strong. He chooses "what is low and despised in the world, even things that are not"—like a forgotten town called Nazareth and an unwed young woman carrying a child conceived without a human father—"to bring to nothing things that are" (1 Corinthians 1:27-28). He humbles the strong and magnifies his strength by exalting the weak. Christmas turns the world upside down.

Hasn't this been our experience of this God and his world? Over and over again, just when we think we have figured him out with our infinitesimally small minds, he shatters our assumptions and plans. He turns our world on its head. Mary's own son will literally embody this peculiar glory of God. And for those of us with eyes to see, like Mary, it is marvelous: the very wisdom of God, worth celebrating in song and in a life of praise.

## GOD MAGNIFIED IN OUR REJOICING

But even before her celebration of God's rescue of the weak, Mary begins with an insight that we should not overlook. Her opening lines not only celebrate *that* God magnifies his strength in the weaknesses of his people but also *how*. How is God magnified in us? Not through human pride and confidence, nor through human wealth and strength, but through the humble heart that rejoices in him.

> *My soul magnifies the Lord, and my spirit rejoices in God my Savior. (Luke 1:46-47)*

This is a life-changing lyric—not just at Christmas but for all of life. God is magnified in his weak people when we, like Mary, rejoice in him. The two are connected. God is shown to be magnificent in Mary as she rejoices in him—because we magnify, or honor, or glorify what or whom we enjoy.

We see a glimpse in Mary's song of what John Piper has called "Christian Hedonism," and its central insight that "God is most glorified in us when we are most satisfied in him." This is not a peripheral truth for Mary, or at Christmas, or at any time of year, but it is endlessly relevant and will be so eternally for God's people as we grow in and expand and deepen our enjoyment of God.

## WHAT CHRISTMAS SINGS ABOUT GOD

We would do well this Advent to listen carefully to Mary's strange song—strange to humans attuned to the music of the world but thrilling to those who have an ear for the God who is, rather than the one of our imaginations.

Neither Mary's song nor Christmas itself is a marginal revelation of the true God. Christmas is a window into his very heart. He does indeed look, with mercy, on those who own their humble estate, to exalt them—while he looks, with terrifying justice, on the prideful, to humble them. And for those of us who are weak and heavy laden, God's ways are marvelous in our eyes and music to our ears.

*Father, you humble the proud and exalt the humble, and we stand in awe. We recognize that the way we feel fragile, exhausted, and burdened this Advent may mean we are right where you want us. You sent your Son to help the weak and weary. Open our eyes to the weaknesses we try to ignore and cover over. In your Son, we are safe to own them, and come humbly to you, to rejoice in you and your strong arms, not ours. Magnify yourself in us this season through our rejoicing in you and your Son. In his name we pray. Amen.*

# 2. THE ETERNITY BEFORE CHRISTMAS

*In the beginning was the Word, and the Word
was with God, and the Word was God. He was
in the beginning with God.*

*John 1:1-2*

The glory of Christmas is that it is not the beginning of Christ. Long before that first Christmas, his story had begun—not just in various prophecies, but in an eternal divine person. Christmas may be the opening of the climactic chapter, but it is certainly not his first.

Christmas *does* mark a conception and birth. We read Mary's magnificent song of submission and of the shepherds' visit to her newborn son. We're told that she "treasured up all these things, pondering them in her heart" (Luke 2:19). For mere humans, such is the stuff of our origins. Prior to our earthly beginnings, we simply did not exist.

But it is not so with the Son of God. His "coming forth is from of old, from ancient days" (Micah 5:2). Unlike every other human birth, the birth celebrated at

Christmas was not a beginning but a becoming. Christmas wasn't his start, but his commission. He was not created; he came.

No other human in the history of the world shares this peculiar glory. As remarkable as his virgin conception is, Christ's *pre-existence* sets him apart even more distinctively. The New Testament makes this pre-existence unmistakable through at least three truths.

## 1. HE EXISTED BEFORE THE INCARNATION

Jesus himself made the stunning claim—so offensive to first-century Jewish people that "they picked up stones to throw at him"—when he said, "Truly, truly, I say to you, before Abraham was, I am" (John 8:58-59). Additionally, four New Testament refrains carry the chorus that the person of Christ existed long before that first Christmas.

### He Came

Mark's Gospel opens under the banner of Jesus as Yahweh himself come to earth (Mark 1:1-3). He came from outside the created realm, into our world, to bring God's long-promised rescue. "The Son of Man came ... to give his life as a ransom for many" (Matthew 20:28; also Mark 10:45; Luke 19:10). In John, the language of coming is descending. "The Son of Man descended from heaven" (John 3:13). Mere humans don't descend; they begin.

Paul and Hebrews follow the same pattern. "Christ came into the world" (Hebrews 10:5), and in one of the most succinct and potent gospel summaries, "Christ Jesus came into the world to save sinners" (1 Timothy 1:15).

## He Became

On its own, "becoming" wouldn't necessitate pre-existence. The key is to ask what he was before he became. He was divinely rich—and became humanly poor (2 Corinthians 8:9). He was in "the form of God"—and then took "the form of a servant" (Philippians 2:6-7). One who was infinitely high because he was God—became a little lower than the angels because he became man (Hebrews 2:9).

His becoming was not a ceasing to be what he had been previously but a taking on (Philippians 2:7) of human flesh and blood. The fully divine Son added full humanity to his person and thus became man as well.

## He Was Sent

The Old Testament prophets were sent without pre-existing but not so with God's own Son. He was sent from outside the world of flesh, into it, to redeem his people. This sending is fundamentally different. In the parable of the tenants, the owner of the vineyard sends his "beloved son" (Mark 12:6) in a way that is decisively distinct from the other servants he had sent previously. "When the fullness of time had come," Paul writes in Galatians 4:4, "God sent forth his Son, born of woman." God didn't take an already-living human and then send him forth into special work; he sent forth his own divine Son to be human.

**He Was Given**

Finally, and perhaps most memorably, the pre-existent Christ was given. "God so loved the world, that he gave his only Son" (John 3:16). The sacrifice of Christ loses its force as an expression of God's love if Jesus did not pre-exist his incarnation. So, also, the "Mount Everest" of biblical promises—Romans 8:32—presupposes the Son's pre-existence in saying that God "did not spare his own Son but gave him up for us all."

## 2. HE EXISTED BEFORE CREATION

But not only did Christ pre-exist that first Christmas; he also pre-existed all creation. The New Testament could not be much clearer on this account. When the Nicene Creed (a churchwide statement of faith from AD 325) confessed that he is "begotten of the Father before all worlds," it did so on the firm foundation of Scripture.

John's Gospel opens with the declaration:

> *In the beginning was the Word, and the Word*
> *was with God, and the Word was God. He was*
> *in the beginning with God. All things were made*
> *through him, and without him was not anything*
> *made that was made. (John 1:1-3)*

Human flesh didn't become the Word. The eternal Word became flesh (John 1:14). So also Colossians 1:16-17:

> *By him all things were created, in heaven and*
> *on earth, visible and invisible, whether thrones*

> *or dominions or rulers or authorities—all things*
> *were created though him and for him. And he*
> *is before all things, and in him all things hold*
> *together.*

So Jesus prays in John 17:5, "Now, Father, glorify me in your own presence with the glory that I had with you before the world existed."

### 3. HE IS PRE-EXISTENT BECAUSE HE IS GOD

That Christ existed before his incarnation, and even before the foundation of the world, is because of his divinity. He is first and last, Alpha and Omega (Revelation 1:8), because he is God. "No formal distinction can be made between deity and pre-existence" (Donald Macleod, *The Person of Christ*, p 57).

Christmas is far more than the celebration of a great man's birth. God himself, in the second Person of the Godhead, entered into our space and into our frail humanity, surrounded by our sin, to rescue us. He came. He became one of us. God sent God. The Father gave his own Son for us and for our salvation.

*Father in heaven, may your Son assume his rightful place in our hearts this Advent. At this most material time of the year in our materialistic society, your Son's pre-existence reminds us of his preciousness over every party and present, over all the trees and trimmings. He is before, and better than, anything in this created world. Cause our hearts to swell in this season at the gift of the person of Christ as our greatest treasure. In his precious name we pray. Amen.*

# 3. THE GLORY OF HIS VIRGIN BIRTH

*The Holy Spirit will come upon you,*
*and the power of the Most High will overshadow you;*
*therefore the child to be born will be called holy—*
*the Son of God.*

*Luke 1:35*

Jesus was born of a virgin. Of the billions of humans who have lived throughout history, only one person entered the world in this way. This is a glory unique to the one God-man. There is only one mediator between God and man (1 Timothy 2:5), and there is only one human who was virgin-born.

Jesus' distinctive birth is no myth or random detail from the Gospels. It is a special honor conferred only on the incarnate Son of God. And it is full of significance for knowing the person of Jesus and God, who has revealed himself in him.

## SUPERNATURAL, NOT MYTHICAL

It was Matthew and Luke who wrote of the virgin conception. We have no good reason to think that either was gullible in the least. Matthew was a former tax-collector and less likely to be deceived than most of us. Luke was a doctor. True, medicine has come a long way in twenty centuries, but it is no recent discovery that virgins don't conceive. As one scholar notes,

> *First-century folk knew every bit as well as we do that babies are produced by sexual intercourse. When, in Matthew's version of the story, Joseph heard about Mary's pregnancy, his problem arose not because he didn't know the facts of life, but because he did.*
> *(N. T. Wright, Who Was Jesus?, p 78)*

Luke even consulted personally with Jesus' mother—he twice records that Mary "treasured up all these things" in her heart (Luke 2:18, 51), reflecting the likelihood that he had had some kind of personal communication with her. She would have been able to confirm or deny that Jesus' birth was supernatural.

## ON GUARD AT THE DOOR OF CHRISTMAS

From the very beginning of Jesus' human life, his eternal Father set him apart as exceptional. Without any compromise of his true humanity, God gave markers that this man was more than mere man. As Donald Macleod writes,

> *The virgin birth is posted on guard at the door of the mystery of Christmas; and none of us*

> *must think of hurrying past it. It stands on*
> *the threshold of the New Testament, blatantly*
> *supernatural, defying our rationalism, informing*
> *us that all that follows belongs to the same order*
> *as itself and that if we find it offensive there is no*
> *point in proceeding further.*
>
> *(The Person of Christ, p 37)*

Blatantly supernatural. Defying our rationalism. And, sadly, a favorite target of modern critical attack in the last two centuries. But it now appears to be more readily embraced today, if only slightly, among the more post-modern types who grant that the birth of the God-man need not be explained by pure naturalism. (One 2003 poll found that 79% of Americans believe in the virgin birth, and even more surprisingly, 27% of self-proclaimed non-Christians affirm the doctrine.)

## WHY THE VIRGIN BIRTH?

But what is the significance of the virgin birth? Why might it be that God chose to do things this way?

To begin with, it highlights the supernatural. At one end of Jesus' earthly life lies his supernatural conception and birth; at the other, his supernatural resurrection and his ascension to God's right hand. At both ends, the God-man's authenticity is attested to by the supernatural working of his Father.

Second, the virgin birth shows that humanity needs a saving that it cannot bring about for itself. The fact that the human race couldn't produce its own redeemer implies that its sin and guilt are profound and that its Savior must come from outside.

Thirdly, in the virgin birth, God's initiative is on display. The angel didn't ask Mary about her willingness. He announced, "Behold, you will conceive in your womb and bear a son, and you shall call his name Jesus" (Luke 1:31). God didn't ask Mary for permission (although she would have readily granted it, Luke 1:38). He acted—gently but decisively—to save his people from their sins (Matthew 1:21).

Finally, this virgin birth hints at the fully human and fully divine natures united in Jesus' one person. The entry of the eternal Word into the world didn't have to happen this way. But it did happen this way. Here's how Wayne Grudem puts it:

> *God, in his wisdom, ordained a combination of human and divine influence in the birth of Christ, so that his full humanity would be evident to us from the fact of his ordinary human birth from a human mother, and his full deity would be evident from the fact of his conception in Mary's womb by the powerful work of the Holy Spirit. (Systematic Theology, p 530)*

God chose to mark the coming of his eternal Son, his specially anointed one, with this extraordinary birth.

## MUST WE BELIEVE IN THE VIRGIN BIRTH?

If God didn't have to send his Son in this way, then is

it important that we believe in the virgin birth? The answer is a resounding yes. It didn't have to happen this way, but God appointed it in this particular way, and chose Matthew and Luke to record it clearly in their Gospels. To deny this doctrine is to open the door to denying anything plainly affirmed in the Bible; as Macleod observes, "Dismissal of the virgin birth is seldom the end of an individual's theological pilgrimage."

Jesus' extraordinary and magnificent virgin birth is well worth contending for. And everything worth contending for is worth rejoicing in. No human has ever existed prior to conception; no other human was virgin-born like this one. This is a unique glory of the God-man.

*Father, we adore your Son. We marvel at his peculiar glory as the God-man, fully divine and fully human, conceived of the Holy Spirit, in one spectacular, pre-existent, incarnate, and now reigning person. Father, in this Advent season, open our eyes to Jesus' glory. As we turn and admire the diamond of his majesty, work within us new heights and depths of love for your Son. In his name we pray. Amen.*

# An Unexpected Child

# 4. WHAT CHILD IS THIS?

*Being found in human form,*
*he humbled himself by becoming*
*obedient to the point of death,*
*even death on a cross.*

*Philippians 2:8*

"What child is this, who, laid to rest on Mary's lap, is sleeping?"

As a child, I was not impressed with a Christmas song that asked a question to which everyone already knew the answer. *What child is this? Really?* It's Jesus of course. We all know that—even the kids know that.

What I didn't then know is that questions aren't just for solving problems and requesting new information. Sometimes questions make a point. We call those "rhetorical questions." At other times the form of a question expresses awe and wonder about something we know to be true, but find almost too good to be true. It's too good to simply say it directly like we say everything else.

When the disciples found themselves in a great windstorm, with waves breaking into the boat, and Jesus spoke a word and calmed the storm, they said to one another, "Who then is this, that even the wind and the sea obey him?" (Mark 4:41). They knew from Scripture that only God himself can still the seas (Psalm 65:7; 89:9; 107:29); this, somehow, had to be God come among them. But it was too wonderful to say. This new revelation of Jesus' glory was too stupendous to keep quiet, and too remarkable not to express in some form. Was indeed God himself in the boat with them? "Who then is this?"

It's in a similar vein that we ask, in song, at Christmas, "What child is this?" We know the answer. It has been plainly revealed. God himself has become man in this child and has come to rescue us. The eternal Word has become flesh to dwell among us (John 1:14). It is clear and certain. We must say it straightforwardly and with courage. And yet it is almost too wonderful to be true. So it is fitting at times like Christmas to wonder, to marvel, to ask in awe, "What child is this?"

## SUCH MEAN ESTATE

What prompts this statement-question of awe, though, is not only that God has become man, but that he has come among us in this way—in this surprising lowliness. The first stanza gives us the glory we expect: "Angels greet" him with "anthems sweet." The heavens are alight with song. That's the kind of arrival we expected.

But even here there's a glimpse of the unexpected. The angels sing *to shepherds*. That's odd. Angels, yes—but shepherds? Shouldn't there be dignitaries, especially from among the regal and religious establishment of the

Jews, who have purportedly long awaited the coming of their Christ? Shouldn't shepherds take a number behind the king and his court, the priests and the scribes, and the Jerusalem elite?

The unexpected is there in the first stanza, but it is the second that turns especially peculiar. "Why lies he in such mean estate, where ox and ass are feeding?" the carol asks. Why indeed? Why in a manger? Why this place of poverty? Why not in a palace, or even a guest room, but in some clearly very lowly structure?

## NAILS, SPEARS
The answer beckons us beyond humble Bethlehem to witness his life of even greater lowliness. And not static lowliness, but increasing lowliness: Jesus, "though he was in the form of God, did not count equality with God a thing to be grasped, but emptied himself, by taking the form of a servant, being born in the likeness of men" (Philippians 2:6-7).

But why? Why this surprising appearance among us? To simply show us it can be done? Surely this is more than a stunt. Why did he come? What was he here to accomplish?

So we press forward in his story, beyond the lowliness of the manger to a life of lowly sacrifice with no place to lay his head (Luke 9:58)—and finally to the ultimate lowliness: when he was condemned unjustly as a criminal, stripped of his garments, and raised up to the most odious of public executions: "… and being found in human form, he humbled himself by becoming obedient to the point of death, even death on a cross" (Philippians 2:8).

Some may suspect that we are souring the brightness and joy of Christmas when we next sing, "Nails, spears shall pierce him through." *Can't we leave that for Good Friday? Let us have our sweet, cuddly baby Jesus at Christmas. No nails, no blood, no death—no thank you.*

But the Word-made-flesh coming without a cross in view is no good news. The light and joy of Christmas are hollow if we sever the link between Bethlehem and Golgotha. "The cross he bore for me, for you." In this first advent, he came not in judgment but mercy.

He did this *for you*. Christmas is *for you* only because his life was for you, and his death was for you, and his triumphant resurrection on the other side was for you. "Nails, spears shall pierce him through" doesn't ruin Christmas. It gives the season its power.

## PEASANTS COME—AND KINGS

In the carol's final verse we sing, "So bring him incense, gold, and myrrh; come peasant, king to own him." Lowly shepherds are here. And when the lofty of his own people will not bow the knee, foreign dignitaries traverse field and fountain, moor and mountain, to honor him by laying down their treasures. Peasants come and kings. The weak and the strong. The wise and the foolish. The low and despised kneel side by side with those who are powerful and nobly born.

The manger is for all sinners because the cross is for all sinners. And this is all too much for simple fact-finding, cool-headed analysis and calculated articulations. This is the stuff of singing. This is the time to say—to declare in the awe and wonder of worship—"What child is this?"

*Father in heaven, we do indeed worship your Son. We bow before him in awe and wonder that he would descend from such heights and that he would go so low, to rescue us. We thank you that he came for both peasants and kings. None of us are too lowly or too exalted to bow the knee this Advent and forever. In Jesus' mighty and merciful name we pray. Amen.*

# 5. THE WORD BECAME FLESH

*The Word became flesh and dwelt among us.*

*John 1:14*

Two big Christmas theology words, among others, are worth knowing. Neither is as difficult as it sounds to unfamiliar ears, though the realities are as profound as anything in the universe.

The first is "incarnation," which refers literally to the *in-fleshing* of the eternal Son of God—Jesus "putting on our flesh and blood" and becoming fully human. The doctrine of the incarnation claims that the eternal second Person of the Trinity took on humanity in the person of Jesus of Nazareth. A helpful way to remember the key aspects of the incarnation is the summary statement of John 1:14: "The Word became flesh."

*The Word* refers to the eternal divine Son, who was "in the beginning with God" and who himself is God (John 1:1). From eternity past, the Son of God has existed in perfect love, joy, and harmony in the fellowship of the Trinity. Like the Father and the Spirit, he is spirit and had no material substance until taking our humanity. But at the incarnation, the eternal Word entered into creation as man. He became a first-century Jew.

*Became* does not mean that he ceased to be God. In becoming man, he did not forsake his divine nature, as if that were even possible. Rather, he became man by taking on human nature in addition to his divine nature. It is essential to the incarnation—and important in all our theology—to recognize that divinity and humanity are not mutually exclusive. The Son of God didn't have to choose between being God and being man. He could be both at the same time. The eternal Word became human, without ceasing to be God.

*Flesh* isn't merely a reference to the human body but the entirety of what makes up humanity—body, mind, emotions, and will. Hebrews 2:17 and 4:15 teach that to save humans Jesus had to be made like us "in every respect" except our sin. In the incarnation, everything proper to humanity was united to the Son of God. The Son of God did not only become like man; he actually became truly and fully human.

## TWO NATURES, ONE PERSON

If the first term, *incarnation*, was familiar, then perhaps the second term, *hypostatic union*, will be less so. But that needn't make it intimidating; its meaning is much easier than it sounds.

Our English adjective "hypostatic" comes from the Greek word *hupostasis*. The early church came to use it as a theological term related to distinctness within the

Trinity—to refer to something like the English word "person."

So in the context of "hypostatic union," hypostatic means personal. The hypostatic union is the personal union of Jesus' deity and humanity—or the one-person union of his two natures.

Jesus has two whole and complete natures—one fully human and one fully divine. What the doctrine of the hypostatic union teaches is that these *two natures* are united in *one person* in the God-man. Jesus is not two persons. He is one person. The hypostatic union is the joining (mysterious as it is to us as mere humans) of the human to the divine in the one person of Christ.

## WHAT IS THE SIGNIFICANCE?

Why bother with this fancy term? At the end of the day, the term itself is not essential, but the concept behind the term is infinitely precious—both in inspiring worship and guarding us from error.

It is immeasurably sweet, and awe-inspiring, to know that Jesus' two natures are perfectly united in his one person. Jesus is not divided. He is not two people. He is one person—one Christ. As the Chalcedonian Creed (a statement issued by a church council in AD 451) declares, his two natures are without confusion, without change, without division, and without separation. Jesus is one.

This means that Jesus is one focal point for our worship. And as Jonathan Edwards famously observed, in this one-person God-man we find "an admirable conjunction of diverse excellencies" which we find in no other person, human or divine.

In other words, because of this hypostatic (one-person) union, Jesus Christ exhibits an unparalleled magnificence for us as humans. No one person satisfies the complex longings of the human heart like the God-man.

God made our human souls in such a way that we will not be eternally content with that which is only human. Finitude cannot slake our thirst for the infinite. And yet, in our finite humanity, we also need a point of contact with the divine. God was glorious long before he became man in Jesus. But we are human, and un-in-carnate deity doesn't connect with us as profoundly as the God who became human. The idea of a God who never became man will not satisfy the human soul like the true God, who did.

## ONE PERSON—FOR US

But beyond just gazing from afar at the spectacular, singular person who is Jesus Christ, we also have in the gospel the amazing revelation that the reason why he became the God-man was *for us*. The personal union of God and man in him is personal for us. His fully human nature joined to his eternally divine nature is permanent proof that Jesus, in perfect harmony with his Father, is unstoppably for us.

The eternal Son of God, without ceasing to be God, took on a fully human nature to his one person, and he has demonstrated his love for us in that while we were still sinners, he died for us (Romans 5:8). Jesus didn't just become man because he could. This was no circus stunt, just for show. He became man, in the words of the ancient creed, "for us and for our salvation."

*Father, we marvel at the singular person of your Son. He was fully divine, in infinite bliss with you, from all eternity, and yet he took on our humanity and subjected himself to the pains and miseries of our sin-sick world "for us and our salvation." Your love for us in and through Christ is far beyond our finding out, but we want to know more. And what we do know is cause for great worship. We worship your Son, dear Father, and long to know and enjoy him more, and all the more in this Advent season. In Jesus' name we pray. Amen.*

# 6. JESUS IS FULLY HUMAN

*In him the whole fullness of deity dwells bodily.*

*Colossians 2:9*

**D**uring Jesus' life on earth, no one questioned his humanity. They saw and heard him for themselves, and touched him, and shared life with him (1 John 1:1). Then the question was: might this man, somehow, someway, be more than human? Could this man, imponderable as it seems, actually be God himself among us?

But for the second generation of Christians, and beyond, it was Jesus' *divinity* that was the given. After all, they worshiped him. Within the church at least, the truth of Jesus' humanity was soon neglected, or even denied (1 John 4:2; 2 John 7).

We must avoid the same mistake. Advent is a ripe opportunity for reflecting on not just the easy parts of the incarnation but also the uncomfortable and challenging aspects of what it means that our Lord is fully human. Not only did the Son of God have—and still has—a fully human body but also a fully human *mind*, *heart*, and *will*.

## HIS HUMAN BODY

The New Testament is clear enough that Jesus has a human body. John 1:14 means at least this, and more: "The Word became flesh."

His humanity became one of the first tests of orthodoxy (1 John 4:2; 2 John 7). He was born (Luke 2:7). He grew (Luke 2:40, 52). He grew tired (John 4:6) and became thirsty (John 19:28) and hungry (Matthew 4:2). He became physically weak (Matthew 4:11; Luke 23:26). He died (Luke 23:46). And he had a real human body, which is now glorified, after his resurrection (Luke 24:39; John 20:20, 27).

## HIS HUMAN EMOTIONS

Throughout the Gospels, Jesus clearly displays human emotions. When he heard the centurion's words of faith, "he marveled" (Matthew 8:10). He says in Matthew 26:38 that his "soul is very sorrowful, even to death." In John 11:33-35, Jesus is "deeply moved in his spirit and greatly troubled," and even weeps. In John 12:27 he says, "Now is my soul troubled," and in John 13:21, he is "troubled in his spirit." The author to the Hebrews writes that "Jesus offered up prayers and supplications, with loud cries and tears" (Hebrews 5:7).

And we dare not overlook the many remarkable expressions of Jesus' joy and rejoicing (Matthew 18:13; 25:21, 23; Luke 10:17-22; 15:5-10; John 15:11; 17:13; Hebrews 1:9; 12:2). As John Calvin memorably summed it up, "Christ has put on our feelings along with our flesh."

## HIS HUMAN MIND

The waters get even deeper. Jesus also has a human mind:

> *Jesus increased in wisdom and in stature and in favor with God and man. (Luke 2:52)*

> *Concerning that day or that hour, no one knows, not even the angels in heaven, nor the Son, but only the Father. (Mark 13:32)*

It may be strange enough to first ponder Jesus, as God, growing and *increasing* in wisdom. Yet so he does, with respect to his humanity. But even more so, the second text is striking for those of us with a high view of Christ. If Jesus is truly God, and God knows everything, how can Jesus not know when his own second coming will be?

The mature answer from church history has been this: in addition to being fully divine, Jesus is fully human. His one person has both an infinite, divine mind and a finite, human mind. He can be said not to know things, as in Mark 13:32, because he is genuinely human and finite— and human minds are not omniscient. *And* Jesus can be said to know all things, as Peter says to him in John 21:17, because he is divine and infinite in his knowledge.

Paradoxical as it is, the Scriptures plainly affirm that Jesus both knows all things as God *and* doesn't know all things as man. For the unique, two-natured, single person of Christ, this is no contradiction but a peculiar glory of the God-man.

## HIS HUMAN WILL

Yet the reality of the human-divine Christ stretches our comprehension even further still. Most difficult of all to grasp, Jesus not only has a divine will but also a human will. Again, the tracks are laid by two key texts:

> *I have come down from heaven, not to do my own will but the will of him who sent me.*
> *(John 6:38)*

> *My Father, if it be possible, let this cup pass from me; nevertheless, not as I will, but as you will.*
> *(Matthew 26:39)*

Jesus has an infinite divine will that is the will of his Father (one will in God). And as man, he has a finite human will that, while being a true human will, is perfectly in sync with, and submissive to, the divine.

These truths are mysterious: beyond our experience and understanding, and beyond what we will ever know as mere humans. But where this leads for those who call him Lord is not finally to confusion but to worship. Jesus is unique and one truly spectacular person. He is fully God. And he is fully man. Would we want to fix our eternal worship and praise on one who was not?

## TRUE HUMAN, TRUE HEALING

Jesus is like us in every respect—human body, heart, mind, and will—except for sin (Hebrews 2:17; 4:15). How amazing that the divine Son of God did not just take on part of our humanity at that first Christmas but all of it—and then took that true humanity all the way to the cross for us, and has now taken it into heaven as our pioneer and into the presence of God.

Jesus took on a human body to save our bodies. And he took on a human mind to save our minds. Without becoming human in his emotions, he could not have rescued ours. And without taking on a human will, he could not have saved our broken and wandering wills. In the words of the fourth-century archbishop Gregory of Nazianzus (329-390), "That which he has not assumed [taken on himself] he has not healed."

He became man in full so that he might save us in full.

*Father, these truths are past finding out. We follow where your word leads, but we don't pretend that our mere human experience can make full sense of it. But as we look at your unique and spectacular Son, the one God-man, we marvel. What a Savior, brother, and friend. This man is indeed worthy of our worship, and as God, he will be the focus of our happy praise forever. In his majestic name we pray. Amen.*

# Unexpected News

# 7. GLORY TO GOD IN THE LOWEST

*In the same region there were shepherds out in the field, keeping watch over their flock by night. And an angel of the Lord appeared to them, and the glory of the Lord shone around them, and they were filled with great fear.*

*Luke 2:8-9*

It may have been the greatest choral presentation in the history of the world. One nameless angel had the honor of singing the lead, with a veritable angelic multitude behind him. But no tickets were sold, and the show was not announced ahead of time. The audience was simply a flock of unresponsive sheep and a lowly band of unsuspecting shepherds. But it was too good to keep quiet about. Word got out, and "all who heard it wondered at what the shepherds told them" (Luke 2:18). The Gospel of Luke records the story for us to wonder at too.

## GOOD NEWS OF GREAT JOY
It had been a night like any other in the fields outside

Bethlehem, so we can imagine the shepherds were seriously caught off their guard when the messenger made his appearance. One old carol describes this moment as angels "sweetly singing o'er the plains"—that may be how the shepherds came to remember the show with nostalgia, but the first surge of emotion that broke in on them was fear. "An angel of the Lord appeared to them, and the glory of the Lord shone around them, and they were filled with great fear" (Luke 2:9).

The angel acknowledges their terror and clarifies that the grandeur of this display—this shining of the glory of God—is not to make these lowly shepherds cower but to make them deeply and enduringly happy. "Fear not, for behold, I bring you good news of great joy that will be for all the people. For unto you is born this day in the city of David a Savior, who is Christ the Lord" (Luke 2:10-11).

This good news of great joy—this declaration designed to make them profoundly and eternally happy—is that, at long last, the long-awaited hope of Israel, the Christ, the anointed One, about whom the prophets have spoken, has finally come. This is his advent, and this is not how anyone was expecting it.

## SEE HIM IN A MANGER LAID

How so? Well for one thing, this grand announcement is happening as a private presentation for unsuspecting shepherds. These are not the kings and rulers, the scribes and Pharisees, the learned and influential and esteemed of the day: precisely the opposite. These men live near the lowest rung; they are the grafters that society takes for granted. They herd sheep.

Here, from the very beginning, as God moves to provide a Savior for all people, he does it not on the world's terms, according to human expectation, but in his own surprising, mysterious, and marvelous way. "God chose what is foolish in the world to shame the wise; God chose what is weak in the world to shame the strong" (1 Corinthians 1:27).

But not only does this extravagant announcement come to lowly shepherds, but the Christ himself comes as a *child*. He is a weak and fragile infant of manifestly humble birth: "You will find a baby wrapped in swaddling cloths and lying in a manger" (Luke 2:12). No castle, no palace, no hospital, not even a house and a crib—he is born into the lowliest of accommodations, wrapped in the most common of raiment, so helpless that he needs to be swaddled to sleep, and laid on hay kept for animals.

## GLORY UP AND DOWN

After the messenger's solo, suddenly the massive choir appears, praising God and saying,

> *Glory to God in the highest, and on earth peace among those with whom he is pleased!*
>
> *(Luke 2:14)*

This impressive presentation is not about the worth and merit of the shepherds. The glory is not theirs.

And it's not about mankind's deservedness and value. This gospel is *for* all people, and this peace is *for* all the earth, and for all those with whom, by faith, God is pleased (Hebrews 11:6)—but this declaration of glory is not *to* them.

Rather, as the angels say, this stunning news, and this strange and wonderful way of carrying it out, is to the glory of God. He is the initiator and enactor. He is the one who has promised this Savior for centuries and has now sent him in humility to shepherds and all who acknowledge their lowliness. It is his goodness on display in this good news, and the great joy he brings adds to the praise that he is given: "Glory to God in the highest." And yes, for the sake of the lowest too.

## CHRIST THE LORD?

Perhaps the most spectacular detail about this spectacular night is this subtle but world-changing line in the angel's declaration: this newborn is "a Savior, who is Christ *the Lord*" (Luke 2:11). Come again? *The Lord?*

It was "an angel of *the Lord*" who appeared, and it was "the glory of *the Lord*" that shone around the shepherds, and when they finally respond, they acknowledge that this is what "*the Lord* has made known to us" (Luke 2:15). And this newborn Christ somehow shares the same divine identity.

Not only was this child sent from the Lord, but this was the Lord himself. Not only had the Lord of heaven initiated and acted to rescue his lowly people from their sin and shame, but he himself had come to earth, wonder upon wonder, and dwelt among us, in our own flesh and blood—the highest made lowest for us.

## COME, ADORE ON BENDED KNEE

The weight and magnitude of it all is too much for the shepherds to take in at once, and even for Mary and Joseph. But the shepherds get the point, and their hearts produce the right impulse, even as their heads are still spinning. They understand that Christmas is not about the worth and goodness of humanity but the mind-blowing mercy of God.

> *And the shepherds returned, glorifying and praising God for all they had heard and seen, as it had been told them. (Luke 2:20)*

*Father in heaven, make us more like these shepherds, glorifying you through our joy in you, and praising you through our words and witness in the world. We don't want to pretend to be strong and wise and noble. We acknowledge our lowliness and marvel that you sent your Son from the heights of heavens to the lowliest of earthly accommodations to announce and accomplish this good news of great joy. In his name we pray. Amen.*

# 8. THE ARRIVAL OF GREAT JOY

*Fear not, for behold, I bring you good news of*
*great joy that will be for all the people. For unto*
*you is born this day in the city of David a Savior,*
*who is Christ the Lord.*

*Luke 2:10-11*

Two years ago, as we unpacked our Christmas boxes and did our annual purge of decorations, our old JOY stocking-holders wound up in the pile for the thrift store. The immediate cause was the arrival of baby Mercy, born earlier that year. Three letters are inadequate to hold four stockings. But perhaps there's also a theological reason to let the JOY holders go: might it be the case that plain "joy" undersells the glory of Christmas? Matthew and Luke accent different aspects of the birth story, but they sing this note in unison: Christ's coming is not simply an occasion for joy but *great joy*.

## GOD'S WORLD OF JOYS
In the beginning, the God of joy made a world of

joys—a creation full of good, altogether "very good," and primed to delight his creatures (Genesis 1:31; 2:9). We too have tasted his goodness in his world, even on this side of sin's curse. We have experienced, however meagerly or infrequently, the blessed emotional surges of God-made delight—in a kind word, in a warm embrace, in our team's victory, in a cool breeze, in good food and drink. We know normal joy.

But Christmas is not normal. Christmas, the Gospels say, is great joy. God set Christmas apart. He himself has come down in the person of his Son. The long-awaited Savior is born. When the angel heralds Christ's arrival, he says, "I bring you good news of *great joy*" (Luke 2:10). And when the wise men travel from afar and find him, "they rejoiced exceedingly with *great joy*" (Matthew 2:10).

This is significant because while the Bible is replete with "joy"—more than two hundred times in an English translation—instances of "great joy" are numbered in single digits. "Great joy" is rare and climactic. At the anointing of King David's own son as his successor, at the height of Israel's kingdom—"great joy" (1 Kings 1:40). At the restoration of the Passover after generations of neglect—"great joy" (2 Chronicles 30:26). At the dedication of Nehemiah's rebuilt walls after the return from exile—"great joy" (Nehemiah 12:43). Joy is the stuff of every day; "great joy" is kept for the highest of moments.

Other than Matthew's and Luke's mentions of "great joy" at Jesus's birth, both Gospels celebrate "great joy" at his resurrection and ascension (Matthew 28:8; Luke

24:52). Acts 15:3 mentions "great joy" at the surprising and wonderful inclusion of the Gentiles in God's new-covenant people, and how else could Jude 24 speak of our coming into God's own presence without describing it as an experience of "great joy"?

## THEN CAME (GREAT) JOY

"Great joy" at Christmas tells us something profound about God and how he works in our world. God gave us a garden in the beginning to prepare us for a garden-city in the end. God made the world to remake it one day. God gave a first covenant to surpass it with a second. God made a world of joys to surpass them all with the treasure hidden in a field and the pearl of great price: and the surpassing value of knowing Christ Jesus our Lord.

God gave us everyday joy to accentuate and deepen the experience of great joy. There must be joy before there can be great joy. We must know good before we can know better. God designed his world of joys to prepare us for great joy in his Son.

How, then, is the joy of Christmas not just normal but great?

## GREAT HEIGHTS

The angel who heralds "great joy" in Luke 2:10 does not come alone: "Suddenly there was with the angel a multitude of the heavenly host praising God and saying, '*Glory to God in the highest*, and on earth peace among those with whom he is pleased!'" (Luke 2:13-14).

Note the great heights of this joy—from the surface of the earth all the way up to the heights of heaven. Such news captures not only lowly shepherds but even the hosts of heaven, who long to look into these things (1 Peter 1:12). And as God's glory rises to the highest places, so does our joy. In both Matthew 2 and Luke 2, "great joy" comes together with worship and praise. "The shepherds returned, glorifying and praising God for all they had heard and seen" (Luke 2:20). The magi "fell down and worshiped him" (Matthew 2:11).

## GREAT LENGTHS

Christmas joy also goes to great lengths. This is "good news of great joy that will be for *all the people*" (Luke 2:10). All the people. Not just kings and high-ranking officials but blue-collar shepherds. Not just Jews, but Gentiles. Black and white. Women and men. Laymen and clergy. Plumbers and dentists. This is no tribal joy quarantined in Jerusalem but great joy extended to all kinds of people, in every place, at every time.

## GREAT DEPTHS

Christmas joy also goes to great depths. Here is a joy deeper than every fear and grief—deeper than every sorrow and pain.

This great joy comes into a world of great sin, great fear, great sorrow, great suffering. In fact, this child, who is joy incarnate, will be a man of sorrows, acquainted with grief, and it will be his great suffering that secures for us the great joy (Isaiah 53:3-6).

From his birth in Bethlehem to his death on a cross, this joy was great enough to endure being born in obscurity and laid in a manger, and having no place to lay his head. He was to be rejected by his own people, delivered over to their authorities, and betrayed by his own friend.

But this great joy could not be extinguished. It cannot. It is too high, too long, too deep—even for death itself. And our joyful Savior is now with us to the end of the age, strengthening us in every fear, cheering us in every grief, holding us in all our suffering. Until the day when he unseats every sorrow, he promises, "No one will take your joy from you" (John 16:22).

*Father in heaven, we thank you for the great joy of Christmas. The coming of your Son, for us and for our salvation, is indeed a cause for great joy—and he himself the greatest of all joys. Father, stir in us in this Advent season a joy in Christ that is increasingly high and wide and deep enough to endure the many trials and sufferings we face in this age. In Jesus' name we pray. Amen.*

# 9. HARK, THE LONG-LOST VERSES SING!

*Suddenly there was with the angel a multitude*
*of the heavenly host praising God and saying,*
*"Glory to God in the highest, and on earth peace*
*among those with whom he is pleased!"*

*Luke 2:13-14*

It's a rare pleasure to find fresh, powerful words to a deeply familiar tune. It might be a newly crafted stanza by a modern writer to accompany an old hymn. Or all-new lyrics to a pre-existing tune. Yet even more delightful, at least to me, is to come into a long-lost stanza by the original writer.

This Advent, perhaps the long-lost stanzas of "Hark! The Herald Angels Sing" can be that for you. But first, let's enjoy the carol from the beginning.

## JOIN THE WELKIN'S SONG
Charles Wesley (1707-1788), brother of John, and one of the greatest hymn-writers in the English language, first published "Hark" in 1739, almost forty years before

American independence. He titled it "Hymn for Christmas Day," and its first couplet read:

> *Hark how all the welkin rings*
> *Glory to the King of Kings*

Welkin is old English for the sky or heavens. So, in modern English: "Listen how all the sky rings." The allusion is to the heavens pulsing with the angelic multitude of Luke's Gospel:

> *Suddenly there was with the angel a multitude of*
> *the heavenly host praising God and saying, "Glory*
> *to God in the highest, and on earth peace among*
> *those with whom he is pleased!" (Luke 2:13-14)*

Wesley's friend, the great evangelist George Whitefield (1714-1770), updated the lyrics almost twenty years later in 1758, giving us the well-known lines:

> *Hark! The herald angels sing*
> *Glory to the newborn King!*

Wesley's original tune was slower and more solemn. Musician William H. Cummings (1831-1915) borrowed a slice of Felix Mendelssohn's 1840 cantata to construct the upbeat carol we know today. The 1961 *Carols for Choirs* collection of Christmas hymns, published by Oxford University, added Whitefield's opening couplet as a refrain after each verse.

## VEILED IN FLESH THE GODHEAD SEE

The carol's first verse is a rousing invitation, to all nations and all nature, to "join the triumph of the skies" and proclaim with the angels that God's long-promised Messiah—his specially anointed One, "the Christ"—is born in Bethlehem.

Who, then, is this Christ? The second verse answers. Ignoble as the birth may seem, he is no ordinary infant. He is "adored" even by highest heaven—and wonder upon wonder, he is the "everlasting Lord": God himself. This is the one of whom the apostle would write, "When the fullness of time had come, God sent forth his Son, born of woman" (Galatians 4:4).

This newborn is God's own Son and God's own self. And he is with us—among us—not by obligation but gladly.

> *Veiled in flesh the Godhead see*
> *Hail the incarnate deity*
> *Pleased as man with man to dwell*
> *Jesus, our Emmanuel*

The third verse, then, marvels at the mission *and sacrifice* of God's Son. In humility, he lays aside the comforts of heaven and takes on our frail humanity—even infancy, even lowly beginnings—in answering the call to our rescue. He is born to die, that we might live. The extent of his descent is matched only by the ascent of grace that we will find in him.

*Mild he lays his glory by*
*Born that men no more may die*
*Born to raise the sons of earth*
*Born to give them second birth*

## LOST VERSES

Wesley's original had fourth and fifth stanzas. Whitefield chose his favorite lines from each and synthesized the fourth and fifth stanzas into one, while *Carols for Choirs* dropped Whitefield's fourth verse altogether, leaving us with the three we typically sing today.

Before ending with Wesley's fourth and fifth stanzas, perhaps I could suggest what we might do with them today, and how to make this little lesson in history and theology a catalyst for worship.

Maybe some worship leader reading this will be inspired to incorporate these rich lines into congregational singing. More of us will have the opportunity to introduce these verses into family singing. Dads in particular can seize upon the opportunity that Christmas gives us to lead in song in the home.

But the simplest application might be to sing these aloud by yourself. Music and song can be powerful means of God's grace. Few of us wring the habit of personal, worshipful singing of its power like we could.

To make these two long-lost verses soar in meaning and power, here are some texts you could meditate on, before using the carol as your prayer for the end of today's reading: for the woman's conquering seed, see

Genesis 3:15; for Christ bruising the serpent's head *in us*, Romans 16:20; for the restoration of ruined nature, Romans 8:19-24. The "mystic union" is our being joined to Jesus by faith; in this union, we belong to him, and he to us; we are his and he is ours (Song of Solomon 2:16; 6:3; 7:10). For Jesus as the second Adam, see Romans 5:12-21 and 1 Corinthians 15:22. For God's restoring us to our original purpose and ultimate destiny by conforming us to his image in Christ, Romans 8:29 and 2 Corinthians 3:18; for Christian maturation as Christ is formed in us, Galatians 4:19.

> *Come, Desire of nations, come*
> *Fix in us thy humble home*
> *Rise, the woman's conqu'ring seed*
> *Bruise in us the serpent's head*
>
> *Now display thy saving pow'r*
> *Ruin'd nature now restore*
> *Now in mystic union join*
> *Thine to ours, and ours to thine*
>
> *Adam's likeness, Lord, efface*
> *Stamp thy image in its place*
> *Second Adam from above*
> *Reinstate us in thy love*
>
> *Let us thee, tho' lost, regain*
> *Thee, the Life, the Inner Man*
> *Oh! to all thyself impart*
> *Form'd in each believing heart*

# Unexpected Guests

# 10. WE THREE KINGS FROM ORIENT AREN'T

*Behold, wise men from the east came
to Jerusalem.*

*Matthew 2:1*

**M**atthew says "behold" to make sure he has our attention. He means for us to be surprised. This is not at all what Mary and Joseph would have expected.

*Magi*, as the wise men are also known, is an ancient word referring to pagan astrologers, from which we get our English word "magic." So while "We Three Kings" is a delightful Christmas carol, these dudes aren't kings. Nor are they political dignitaries but pagan specialists in the supernatural, akin to what we might call sorcerers and wizards—and they are coming to worship Jesus.

We really should beware of having a narrower vision of who can come to Jesus than God does. We might be prone to write off people like this, but God isn't. He draws. He woos. He calls out for himself, and his Son, worshipers from the most unexpected of places.

## MAGIC IN THE BIBLE

The magi are unexpected partly because the Old Testament so clearly condemns their craft. Moses had been met by court magicians in Egypt (Exodus 7:22; 8:7, 18-19; 9:11) and later clearly condemned the use of such magic in Deuteronomy 18:9-14. The prophets Isaiah (47:11-15) and Jeremiah (10:1-2) added their words of judgment on those dabbling in magic and sorcery. Magi were "the magicians, the enchanters, the sorcerers, and the Chaldeans" that the pagan king of Babylon commanded to tell him his dreams in Daniel 2:2.

The New Testament also joins the refrain in Acts 8, when Peter rebukes a man named Simon, who trafficked in magic and offered money to obtain the apostles' power to heal, and in Acts 13:6-12, as Paul denounces a magician named Elymas, who was opposing the advance of the gospel. So also John's vision at the end of Revelation twice lists sorcerers as among those who are cast out of the new creation into the lake of fire (Revelation 21:8; 22:15).

The whole Bible, Old Testament and New, plainly condemns the kind of astrology, stargazing, and dabbling in the dark arts typical of the magi. In biblical terms, the magi are plainly marked as "sinners."

So, "we three kings of orient" aren't kings, but they do come to worship Jesus, the true King: "And going into the house [the magi] saw the child with Mary his mother, and they fell down and worshiped him. Then, opening their treasures, they offered him gifts, gold and frankincense and myrrh" (Matthew 2:11).

## ISAIAH'S PROPHECY

Some, at this point, speculate as to the symbolism of the gifts: gold represents Jesus as king, frankincense as priest, and myrrh as our sacrifice. Perhaps. However, the main connection Matthew would have us make—by pairing gold and frankincense—is to Isaiah 60, where Isaiah prophesies about all the nations coming to Israel's king (see also Psalm 72:10-11):

> *Nations shall come to your light, and kings to the brightness of your rising. Lift up your eyes all around, and see; they all gather together, they come to you; your sons shall come from afar ["bearing gifts we traverse far"?] ... The wealth of the nations shall come to you. A multitude of camels shall cover you, the young camels of Midian and Ephah; all those from Sheba shall come. They shall bring gold and frankincense, and shall bring good news, the praises of the LORD. (Isaiah 60:3-6)*

This Christ is not only the king of Israel. He is the king of all nations: the King of kings. Kings in their own right will come to bow at the feet of this king, and they will bring their treasures as freewill offerings in worship—their wealth, their best cultural products and practices, of which gold and frankincense are just the beginning.

## THE APOSTLE JOHN'S VISION

Revelation 21 picks up on Isaiah 60 and recasts this prophetic vision of the future with Jesus at the center.

> *I saw no temple in the city, for its temple is the
> Lord God the Almighty and the Lamb. And the
> city has no need of sun or moon to shine on it,
> for the glory of God gives it light, and its lamp is
> the Lamb. By its light will the nations walk, and
> the kings of the earth will bring their glory into
> it, and its gates will never be shut by day—and
> there will be no night there. They will bring into
> it the glory and the honor of the nations.*
> *(Revelation 21:22-26)*

The nations bring their best. Gentile kings will gladly
bow to the Jewish King of all kings. And not only will
the glory of God light the whole kingdom, but the
single lamp that illumines all will be the Lamb—the
Lamb who was slain for us.

## JEWISH KING, SAVIOR OF THE GENTILES

When the magi came to Jerusalem asking, "Where is
he who has been born king of the Jews?" little did they
know that they were asking for him by the very title that
would be written above his head as he hung on the cross
dying for sins that were not his own: "The king of the
Jews" (Matthew 27:37).

This true king of the Jews is not a usurping king like
Herod, abusing power, acting impulsively, and employ-
ing deceit to bolster his crushing grip on the throats
of his subjects. Rather, this king of the Jews is the one
true king, who "came not to be served but to serve,
and to give his life as a ransom for many" (Matthew

20:28). He's the ruler who doesn't merely demand our homage but wins it with his shocking self-giving on our behalf—all the way to death, even death on a cross. He is the king who demonstrates his love for his people in that while we were still sinners—engaged in our own equivalents of stargazing and wizardry—he died for us (Romans 5:8).

This side of the cross we know more than the magi knew. Not only would this God graciously draw Gentile sinners to himself and permit them to come near to his Son, but he would provide eternal salvation for astrologer-sinners like them, and sinners like us too, through the willing death of that very child they came to honor.

*Father in heaven, we remember that we were at one time separated from Christ, alienated from your people and strangers to your covenants, having no hope and without you in the world (Ephesians 2:12). But now, O God, in Christ Jesus, we who once were far off, like magi, have been brought near by the blood of Christ (Ephesians 2:13). Christmas is a tribute to your grace, not our deservedness. Advent marks your coming in Christ to pluck us from our sin, and only then our coming to Christ to bow the knee in worship. He came not to call the righteous but sinners. We own our rebellion and many failures, and gladly bow before your Son. In his name we pray. Amen.*

# 11. THE IRONY OF
# THE EPIPHANY

*Herod summoned the wise men secretly and
ascertained from them what time the star had
appeared. And he sent them to Bethlehem, saying,
"Go and search diligently for the child, and when
you have found him, bring me word, that I too
may come and worship him."*

*Matthew 2:7-8*

January 6 has long been the date when the West-
ern church has observed the Feast of the Epiphany. From the Greek for "appearance" or "manifesta-
tion" (*epiphaneia*), Epiphany celebrates the appearance
of the Son of God among us as one of us—both fully
divine and fully human—and marks the end of "the
twelve days of Christmas" that follow Advent, beginning on December 25.

In particular, Epiphany has become identified with
the arrival of the magi, those pagan astrologers who
make their own surprising appearance in Matthew 2 to
worship baby Jesus.

We've already seen how striking it is in Matthew 2 that the religiously uncouth magi seek to worship the newborn Jewish king; but equally striking is that the religious leaders of the day do not. Pagan astrologers bow the knee (v 10-11), while the Jerusalem religious elite turn their back (v 3-8). This is the great irony in the Epiphany.

## AN EASY ANSWER FOR THE RELIGIOUS

As the story continues, Herod's wickedness becomes apparent enough. Insecure, disturbed, deceitful, murderous—despite his sincere-sounding words to the magi, he does not really intend to honor the child but to kill him. But the subtle sin of the religious leaders in the previous verses is perhaps just as sinister, if not more so.

Verse 4 says that Herod assembled "all the chief priests [Sadducees] and scribes [Pharisees] of the people, [and] he inquired of them where the Christ was to be born." Here gather the trained theologians of the day. They know the biblical concepts and technical terms. They've deeply studied the Hebrew Scriptures—and memorized them. "Where is the Messiah to be born?" It's a piece-of-cake answer for these guys: *Bethlehem. Check Micah.*

## STRANGE INDIFFERENCE

What is so tragic is that they know the answer, but none of them acts on it. None of these trained theologians, so far as we know, go to Bethlehem. Dirty shepherds leave their flocks and seek out a baby in a manger. Pagan astrologers traverse afar, for hundreds of miles and months on the road. Meanwhile, the religious leaders, full of insider knowledge and Bible jargon and pat answers, don't bother to make the relatively short five-mile journey to Bethlehem to actually see this child for which all their theological classes should have prepared them.

Matthew commentator David Turner calls it "the strange indifference" of these theological-answer guys, who have amassed loads of biblical knowledge but don't act on it. Their heads are filled with verses, doctrines, and religious facts, but their hearts reject the very Messiah to which their training should have pointed them.

## THE DANGER OF MERE RELIGION

Is the warning here not obvious for those of us who have taken class after class and read Christian book after Christian book? Many of us are all too familiar with church jargon. We have learned how to say all the right things to appear pious. We've memorized some Scriptures. We know how to sound Christian in our repeated use of precious theological terms and concepts. But biblical training does not guarantee that our hearts incline toward worshiping the true king. Religious language and learning can cloak an infatuation with the kingdom of self.

Note the contrast between the pagan astrologers and the religious establishment. The magi don't know much, but they rejoice exceedingly with great joy (v 10) at the true revelation from God they have received. Meanwhile the religious leaders who know lots—who have all the answers and books about books about books—are disturbed along with Herod and refuse to submit to the long-awaited king (v 3).

This well-informed rejection of Jesus by the religious establishment was a pattern that would repeat throughout his life and culminate in his death. "The religious leaders," writes Turner, "replete with scriptural knowledge, react with apathy here and with antipathy later [when they crucify Jesus]" (*Matthew*, Baker Exegetical Commentary on the New Testament, p 87). Likewise, the *Africa Bible Commentary* astutely observes,

> *The successors of these [religious] experts would be at odds with the adult Jesus, and in the end they would conspire to put him to death. The most knowledgeable church people often include those who take Jesus for granted. It is a dangerous situation to be in. It is no less a sin than the outright hatred of Herod, for in the end it leads to the same destiny (where Herod failed to kill the baby Jesus, the chief priests succeeded). Our pride in our knowledge of Christ, the Bible, and the church may turn out to be a snare in the end.*
> *(p 1111)*

## FOR THE RELIGIOUS AND THE MAGI

In this tragic disinterest in and rejection of their own Messiah, we find a warning to the modern-day Pharisee in all of us: Bible knowledge, acquired from all our classes and gleaned from all our books, can be precious fuel for worshiping the true Jesus or a deceptive excuse for keeping Jesus at arm's length. Increased knowledge doesn't necessarily translate into increased worship. Don't take Jesus for granted.

With this warning, we also hear an invitation to those more like the magi: the non-churched "pagans" and de-churched disenfranchised. You may not have any Christian background (or you did and rejected it, maybe because of the religious types above). You may not know much Christian jargon. You don't fit nicely into the church-goer box, and yet you're being drawn to Jesus. The whole Christian scene may feel really foreign to you. But we want you with us. We want the "magi." Please don't let imperfect Christians scare you away from our perfect Christ.

*Father, here, almost halfway through Advent, we check our hearts. Advent is not for the mere increase of knowledge. Advent is for adoring your Son. Remove whatever barriers in us are keeping us from falling to our knees with the magi. Forbid that we would stand idly by, puffed up in our seeming knowledge, yet unwilling to come and worship. Save us from the traps of man-made religion and its pride, and give us the humble desperation of worshipers who don't pretend to be worthy. In Jesus' name we pray. Amen.*

# 12. EXCEEDING GREAT JOY

*When they saw the star, they rejoiced exceedingly with great joy. And going into the house, they saw the child with Mary his mother, and they fell down and worshiped him. Then, opening their treasures, they offered him gifts, gold and frankincense and myrrh.*

*Matthew 2:10-11*

Advent is not just about acknowledging Jesus in our waiting but adoring him. Christmas is not first about witness but about worship. So in the words of a well-loved carol of the same name, "Come, all ye faithful." Come, "joyful and triumphant." "O come, let us adore" our Christ.

But beware your standard of who can come in worship. As we've seen, at Jesus' own birth, it wasn't the seemingly squeaky-clean religious elites who bowed the knee in worship. Instead they stood aloof with apathy, while the apparently uncouth streamed in to adore him.

## ALL YE FAITHFUL

We need look no further than the magi of Matthew 2 to recalibrate our understanding of what the carol describes as the "faithful." To call them "three kings" is overstated. "Wise men" is positive spin. These guys are more like sorcerers. They are stargazers watching for who knows what in the skies, rather than looking into the Scriptures, and God in his grace comes to them through the very channel of their sin. Even here at Jesus' birth, he is making wizards into worshipers worldwide. He is claiming sheep even from the priestly caste of pagan religion.

Don't miss the message of the magi: if such sinners as these can approach the Christ and fall down in worship, so may all—so may we. Pagan astrologers prostrate in adoration is a stunning emblem announcing that all sinners are welcome, to bow in worship and be changed. Who are we to turn others away?

## JOYFUL AND TRIUMPHANT

You may know the well-worn lines from Matthew 2:10-11. But let's travel these trails again as the magi adore the Jewish Messiah. Matthew piles up the joy language so that we don't miss it. The magi didn't just rejoice, but did so *exceedingly*. And added to that, they did so not just "with joy" but with "*great* joy."

Perhaps we assume that the shepherds in Luke 2 would have been the more emotional types, while these erudite pagan astrologers would have been more inclined to keep calm and collected. But the joy language here in Matthew 2 is conspicuous—even arresting—exploding with even greater gusto than in Luke 2, when the angels announced "good news of a great joy that will be for all the people" (Luke 2:10), and the shepherds "returned, glorifying and praising God for all they had heard and seen" (Luke 2:20). Here our wicked wizards, Matthew says, "rejoiced exceedingly with great joy."

## COME AND BEHOLD HIM
Such unexpected joy is not disconnected from their worship of the baby Jesus. Exceeding great joy is the heart of true adoration. The essence of worship is not physical actions and mere external motions of homage. At its heart, worship is in "spirit and truth," as Jesus says in John 4—truths about him and a spirit of great joy in him. It is spiritually looking to Jesus and *rejoicing exceedingly with great joy.*

But is that what is meant when Matthew says the magi "worshiped" this child? Did they know that this, in fact, was God himself, who had come in the flesh? Were they worshiping this child as the God-man? Perhaps they were merely paying homage to one whom they anticipated would be a great earthly king. Maybe that's what they understood of the Balaam prophecy in Numbers 24:17, "A star shall come out of Jacob, and a scepter shall rise out of Israel." Maybe the magi subscribed to a tradition informed generations before by Jewish exiles in Babylon.

But it seems more is going on here than simply honoring a future earthly king. If by "worship," Matthew merely means that they paid him homage, as subjects pay homage to their king, then it seems odd that they had traveled so far, and redundant to say "they fell down." Falling down is the physical posture, but the word "worship" denotes something more. Worship arises from and centers in the heart. The magi recognize this newborn as a king who will reign not only over Israel but the whole world, thus making them his subjects even though they aren't Israelites.

## GOLD, FRANKINCENSE, AND MIRTH

That said, the magi are worshiping better than they know, at least in some sense. In chapter one, Matthew has already told us of the virgin conception and that this baby is called "Immanuel, God with us" (Matthew 1:23) and will save his people from their sins (Matthew 1:21). And in the rest of his Gospel, Matthew will unfold the surprising story of how this child, born a king, will walk an excruciating path to his cosmic reign—a path literally excruciating (a word from the Latin *crux*, for cross) as he is nailed to a Roman cross on his path to glory.

And since we Christians now know more, we have all the more reason to adore him. May we come to Christmas with no less joy than these enthusiastic magi. Certainly our Advent worship is more that of these stargazing "wise men" than it is that of the scrupulous Jerusalem religious elite, who knew their Scriptures, but wouldn't bow the knee. We come as sinners, struggling, unclean, unimpressive—veritable "astrologers."

But that doesn't mean we come joylessly. Why? Because Jesus is marvelously merciful grace incarnate (Titus 2:11). Because Jesus came to seek and save lost magi (Luke 19:10), to heal the sick and call sinners (Matthew 2:17), to serve the spiritually broken (Mark 10:45), and to destroy the works of the devil (1 John 3:8). So we come to him, "joyful and triumphant." We sinners come, even in stargazing rebellion so great as ours, and we adore Christ the Lord with joy—rejoicing exceedingly with great joy.

*Father in heaven, as we come and we wait in this Advent season, we long to be appropriately joyful and triumphant. We do not want to be chipper or emotionally thin or triumphalistic. Nor do we want to underappreciate the glory of your own Son coming among us. Father, grant that we may be more like the magi—that we rejoice, and do so exceedingly, and with great joy. And give us, in such joy, rooted in the security of your own Son, the wherewithal to endure the waves of pain that will come or are already upon us. Great joy does not mean no sorrows. But it does mean you have prepared us for them and will keep us in them. In Jesus' name we pray. Amen.*

# The Unexpected Town

# 13. JESUS OBEYED HIS PARENTS

*He went down with them and came to Nazareth
and was submissive to them.*

*Luke 2:51*

By the end of Luke 2, we're no longer reading about
baby Jesus. He is twelve years old (Luke 2:42), on
the cusp of adulthood in the ancient world.

Likely, Jesus was already more competent in the faith
than his parents. After all, he was not only "filled with
wisdom" (Luke 2:40) but also "without sin" (Hebrews
4:15). That he eclipsed his parents in spiritual and theological competency, however, didn't put him in charge.
Not yet. How impressive would his emerging understanding have been if he had overlooked the commandment to "honor your father and your mother" (Exodus
20:12)? And so Luke tells us that Jesus was "submissive
to them" (Luke 2:51).

Here Jesus, at age twelve, teaches us an essential lesson
for any age: godly submission, in whatever context, does
not stem from lack of competency. We are never too

smart, too skilled, too experienced, or too spiritual for God-given submission.

None of this means Jesus' human obedience was automatic. Godly submission doesn't happen without effort—first from parents and then from their child. It is learned. Just as Jesus "learned obedience [to his heavenly Father] through what he suffered" (Hebrews 5:8), so he also learned it by Joseph's patience and attention.

## LIMITS OF EARTHLY SUBMISSION

His submission to his parents did have limits. In Luke 2 we come within earshot of this tension. The twelve-year-old boy and his parents have been to Jerusalem for the Passover, but on the journey home Jesus is discovered to be missing. When, after three days of frantic searching, they finally find him in the temple, Mary, exasperated, says, "Son, why have you treated us so? Behold, *your father* and I have been searching for you in great distress" (Luke 2:48). Jesus responds, "Why were you looking for me? Did you not know that I must be in *my Father's* house?" (Luke 2:49). His parents, we're told, did not understand "the saying" at the time (Luke 2:50), but it shouldn't be lost on us now.

Jesus' highest and final submission was to heaven. Submission on earth, however proper, would not keep him from obeying his Father, dwelling in his Father's house, or even parting from his parents for three days. His Father in heaven was the sole recipient of his absolute allegiance, even as his father and mother on earth received his real and substantial respect.

## GLIMPSES OF GOD AND MAN

Yet the place in the story where we most glimpse the twelve-year-old Christ's "admirable conjunction of diverse excellencies," as Jonathan Edwards (1703-1758) put it, may be in Luke 2:46-47:

> *After three days they found him in the temple,*
> *sitting among the teachers, listening to them*
> *and asking them questions. And all who heard*
> *him were amazed at his understanding and his*
> *answers.*

This is no small tribute to both his parents' diligence and the Spirit's power. We see his true humanness as he listens and asks questions. He has questions because he is human. He's growing. He's learning. He's humble enough to listen, and to admit what he doesn't know by asking questions. And in it all, he is stunningly submissive.

But he doesn't only have questions. He has enough backbone to speak. And when he did, "all who heard him were amazed at his understanding and his answers." He spoke up because his Father had spoken. God had revealed himself in the prophets, and preserved it in writing. His Father had not been silent, and so the Son (and we ourselves, if we've listened) was not without understanding and answers.

## NOT SO AMONG YOU

A day was coming when all things would be subjected to him (1 Corinthians 15:28), but first his Father would have him learn what it meant to be subject himself. First, he would learn "from the bottom" the beauty and joy of God-designed submission. Then he would know, and display, "from the top" the true heart of leading like his Father: not lording it over those in his charge (Mark 10:42; 1 Peter 5:3), not being served but serving (Mark 10:44-45), not squashing his subjects but working with them for their joy (2 Corinthians 1:24; Hebrews 13:17).

The God-man leads as one who knows what it's like to follow. He wields all authority in heaven and on earth as one who knows what it means to submit, on earth, to his fellow man. He learned first to obey his parents before others were called to obey him. So also his people—Christians, little christs—he calls, under his lordship, to be "submissive to rulers and authorities" (Titus 3:1; also Romans 13:1, 5; 1 Peter 2:13), and in church life to "be subject to the elders" (1 Peter 5:5). And just as Jesus's submission prepared him to shepherd, the same is true for his flock. Angels and the world to come will be subject to his sheep (1 Corinthians 6:3; Hebrews 2:5).

## ONE STEP AT A TIME

At age twelve, Jesus is not yet carrying his own cross-beam to Golgotha. But as he obeys his parents and returns with them from Jerusalem, he walks the path that will eventually lead him back there. His own self-humbling—which began in coming as an infant and now extends in submitting to his parents—will culminate "by becoming obedient to the point of death, even death on a cross" (Philippians 2:8). So even here in Luke 2 he walks the terrifying and glorious path that lies before him, one act of obedience at a time.

Yet under his Father's strong hand, his story of descent would not end with his death. The Father would not leave his Son in the grave but would highly exalt him (Philippians 2:9). This is where godly obedience always leads, in God's good timing. In obeying his earthly parents, Jesus humbled himself under the mighty hand of his heavenly Father, and *at the proper time*, God raised him up (1 Peter 5:6; James 4:10).

Jesus' obedience did not spell the end of his happiness; nor will ours. Rather, his obedience was the death of everything that would have kept him from full and lasting joy.

*Father, we marvel at this "admirable conjunction" in your Son: fully God, yet fully man, and submissive to his human parents. Asking questions to grow in his understanding, and humbly formulating answers because you have spoken. Father, give us, like your Son, the humility of submission to the human authorities you've given us. May we, like him, know that the path of glad submission is the path of full and lasting joy. In Jesus' name we pray. Amen.*

# 14. GOD GREW UP IN A FORGOTTEN TOWN

*He went down with them and came to Nazareth
and was submissive to them.*

*Luke 2:51*

The Old Testament never mentioned Nazareth.

It's peculiar, in a way. Think of all the genealogies and historical accounts, and what seems, at least to us today, like unusual attention to land, geography, and location. So many place names—and yet not one single mention of a rustic settlement tucked away in a region—Galilee—known for its obscurity.

Nazareth was an uncelebrated, forgotten town, off the beaten path, even for Galilee. When guileless Nathanael queried a friend about Jesus, he expressed the common Jewish sentiment in the first century (John 1:46): "Can anything good come out of Nazareth?"

Yet here in this sleepy town, Jesus' story began, and returned (Luke 1:26; 2:51). His family were Nazarenes. And it was only a matter of time before it would be the moniker that his enemies, and the demons besides, would use to cast aspersions on his credibility: "Jesus of Nazareth."

## THIRTY YEARS IN OBSCURITY

Today we sing about the "little town" of Bethlehem, but Bethlehem, humble as it was compared to Jerusalem, had a name that dwarfed Nazareth's. Bethlehem was a city, with a history, and "the city of David" at that. Yet while Jesus was born in noble Bethlehem, Mary and Joseph came there only as census travelers. It was not where the family would stay. After they took their child up to Jerusalem to dedicate him, "they returned into Galilee, to their own town of Nazareth" (Luke 2:39).

So also, after Jesus' memorable visit to the temple at age twelve, Luke tells us that he "went down" from Jerusalem with his parents. Indeed he did. To leave Jerusalem was to *go down*—not just geographically but socially. And yet, as a glimpse into the self-emptying pattern of his incarnation, the *Son of God* "went down with them and came to Nazareth" (Luke 2:51).

Outside the New Testament references, we know very little, if anything, that is reliable about ancient Nazareth—because it was so obscure. Eminent first-century figures didn't know or speak much about it, at least not in publications prominent enough to be preserved. Outside Israel, the town was simply unknown: which is why the Gospel writers had to explain what Nazareth was—a town in Galilee—when they first mentioned it (Matthew 2:23; Mark 1:9; Luke 1:26).

Still, in God's wise, world-shaming plan for his Son, part of his life of humility and submission to his parents was to leave the buzzing, big-city temple—the very nexus of the nation's activity and excitement—and *go down* to small-town Nazareth, to live for thirty years in obscurity. Here he would remain until John the Baptist's arrest (Matthew 4:13). And Nazareth not only meant a more out-of-the-way, rural, even backwater life than "up" in Jerusalem, but "Nazarene" would be a stigma he would carry for the rest of his life.

*Can anything good come out of Nazareth?*

## "JESUS OF NAZARETH"

During his earthly life, so far as we know, Jesus never self-identified as "Jesus of Nazareth." Only rarely did his followers call him that (John 1:45). Typically, it was crowds who were unfamiliar with him that did so (Matthew 21:11; 26:71; Mark 10:47; Luke 18:37). Or his foes: demons (Mark 1:24; Luke 4:34), false witnesses (Acts 6:14), and the soldiers who came with the traitor to arrest him (John 18:5, 7). And while many disparaged him for his hometown, even his fellow Nazarenes soon rejected him, drove him out of town, and threatened to throw him off a cliff (Luke 4:28-30).

Wherever we find his name on the lips of foes who want to give it a derogatory spin, expect them to call him "Jesus of Nazareth." And if Nathanael's comment, and the venom of demons and detractors, had not been enough, Pilate inscribed it on the instrument of his torture: "Jesus of Nazareth, the King of the Jews" (John

19:19). He humbled himself to the point of death, even death on a cross, even as a Nazarene.

## THE GLORY OF NAZARETH

Yet Nazareth's story did not end in dishonor. The Father saw fit not only to redeem a fallen race but also a disgraced moniker when he raised the Nazarene from the dead. Now the risen Christ is indeed "Jesus of Nazareth"—not in shame but in unparalleled glory.

First it came from the angel at the tomb: "Do not be alarmed. You seek Jesus of Nazareth, who was crucified. He has risen; he is not here" (Mark 16:6). For more than three decades, "Nazarene" had been a bitter foretaste of his coming crucifixion. Now the tables had turned. Now it tasted of divine glory.

After Jesus' ascension, the tagline became a fixture in Peter's ministry. The crucified, risen Lord of the universe was none other than "Jesus of Nazareth" (Acts 2:22). Peter healed a lame man "in the name of Jesus of Nazareth" (Acts 3:6) and declared the name to all who would listen (Acts 4:10). Even in Caesarea he came preaching to the Gentiles of God's anointing on "Jesus of Nazareth" (Acts 10:38).

Then came the revelation to Saul of Tarsus, who would later admit, "I myself was convinced that I ought to do many things in opposing the name of Jesus of Nazareth" (Acts 26:9). Here even Jesus himself—in the only record we have of him self-identifying with Nazareth—took up the newly honorific title when he appeared on the Damascus road in a vision to Saul, saying,

"I am Jesus of Nazareth, whom you are persecuting" (Acts 22:8).

## GOD GREW UP IN NAZARETH

God himself grew up in a forgotten town in Galilee. He came down from Jerusalem, and went down in self-humbling, and down into the tomb, and then took Nazareth up with him in his triumph.

*Can anything good come out of Nazareth?* The answer to Nathanael's question is an emphatic *yes*. And not only good but the greatest. And because our God loves to produce his best in the places we least expect, perhaps we shouldn't be so surprised when he makes the forgotten places in our stories into his chosen channels of our greatest good.

*Father, we believe you are sovereign over, and present in, the most modest and uninteresting aspects of our lives. Forgive our disdain for the things you have ordained for us. Banish from us any lust for the limelight that would send us running from our Nazareth, prematurely angling for Jerusalem. Father, grant us the faith and patience to live with joy in the callings you've given us, as we marvel at the faith and patience of your Son, in whose name we pray. Amen.*

# 15. HOW GOD BECAME A MAN

*The child grew and became strong, filled with wisdom. And the favor of God was upon him. … Jesus increased in wisdom and in stature and in favor with God and man.*

*Luke 2:40, 52*

It is striking how little we know about most of Jesus' life on earth. Between the events surrounding his celebrated birth and the beginning of his public ministry when he was "about thirty years of age" (Luke 3:23), few details have survived.

Given the influence and impact of his life, humanly speaking we might find it surprising that so little about his childhood, adolescence, and early adulthood is available. That is, unless, divinely speaking, this is precisely how God would have it. But why?

## DEVELOPMENT DIGNIFIED

The Gospel of Luke captures three decades of the most important human life in the history of the world in remarkably simple terms. After the high angelic announcement

to lowly shepherds (Luke 2:8-21) and the young family's first visit to the temple (Luke 2:22-38), Luke then
summarizes Jesus' first twelve years of life in astonishing
modesty:

> The child grew and became strong, filled with
> wisdom. And the favor of God was upon him.
> *(Luke 2:40)*

Then, after recounting the story of the twelve-year-old
Jesus impressing adults at the temple (Luke 2:41-51),
Luke reports on some two decades—well more than
half the God-man's dwelling among us—in this simple
sentence:

> *Jesus increased in wisdom and in stature and in
> favor with God and man. (Luke 2:52)*

How fascinating it would be to know what life was like
for the boy Jesus. Did he plainly outpace his peers in
learning? How often did his sinlessness infuriate fallen
siblings? How skilled was he as a worker? How "perfect"
was his carpentry, or did it make perfect sense around
town when he transitioned into public ministry?

But it's easy to digress into speculation and miss the
powerful point of these important summary verses in
Luke. God has something to teach us here in the precious
few details. That he would send his own Son to live and
mature and labor in relative obscurity for some three
decades, before "going public" and gaining recognition,

has something to say to us about the dignity of ordinary human life and labor—and the sanctity of slow, incremental growth and maturation.

God could have sent forth a full-grown Christ. Not only that, but from the beginning he could have created a world of static existence: a world without infants, children, awkward teens, middle-agers, and declining seniors—just a race of young, spry, "mature" adults. But God didn't do it that way. And he doesn't do it that way today. Even apart from the effects of sin, God designed us for dynamic existence, for stages and seasons of life, for growth and development in body and in soul, both toward others and toward God.

Luke's understated summary of the greater part of Jesus' earthly life powerfully dignifies the everyday "growing pains" common to humanity.

## JESUS GREW IN STATURE

As we've already seen, Jesus is both "truly God and truly man, *of a reasonable soul and body*" (Chalcedon, AD 451). Having a "true human body," Jesus was born, he grew, he thirsted, he hungered, he wept, he slept, he sweated, he bled, and he died.

All four Gospels unfold his three-year public ministry, and give nearly half their space to the final week of his life. But what was the God-man doing during most of his earthly life? He was growing. What did he do for three decades between his celebrated birth and his unforgettable ministry? He walked the ordinary, unglamorous path of basic human maturation. He grew.

The man Christ Jesus did not simply emerge from the wilderness preaching the kingdom. He learned to latch and crawl, to walk and talk. He scraped his knees. Perhaps he broke a finger or wrist. He fought off viruses, suffered through sick days, and navigated his way in the awkwardness of adolescence. He learned social graces and worked as a common laborer in relative obscurity for more than half his earthly life.

## JESUS GREW IN WISDOM

But Jesus grew not only in body but also in soul; like every other human, he grew in wisdom and knowledge. Even by age twelve, Luke could say Jesus was "filled with wisdom" (Luke 2:40), not because he got it all at once, or had always had it, but because he was learning (Luke 2:52).

Through sustained effort and hard work, he came into mental acumen and emotional intelligence that he did not possess as a child. His human mind and heart developed through the painful steps of regular progress. He matured mentally and emotionally, just as he grew physically.

It's true that later in his life there were instances of supernatural knowledge, given by the Spirit, in the context of ministry. He knew Nathanael before he met him (John 1:47), and that the Samaritan woman had had five husbands (John 4:18), and that Lazarus had died (John 11:14). But we shouldn't confuse such supernatural knowledge, given by special revelation, with the hard-earned, finite learning of his upbringing.

Jesus learned from the Scriptures, and from his mother, in community and in the power of the Holy

Spirit, and he increased in wisdom by carefully observing everyday life and how to navigate God's world.

## IN FAVOR WITH GOD AND MAN

Finally, we're told, Jesus increased "in favor with God and man." It's a deliberate echo of the words of 1 Samuel 2:26: "Now the boy Samuel continued to grow both in stature and in favor with the Lord and also with man." And it also serves an important point: true human growth is not Godward at the expense of our fellow humans. And development in concern for others should not serve as a distraction from Godward advance. The first commandment is to love God. And the second is like it: love your neighbor as yourself.

No human, not even the God-man himself, skips the growth and maturation process, with all the attendant pains; and no true growth is one-dimensional but toward both God and man.

*Father, grant that we do not begrudge you the glory of our long, arduous maturation processes. As we stumble, and even flounder, in our awkward stages and hardest moments, we are tasting the growing pains that your Son knows well. And he stands ready to help us persevere until your process is complete. So we lean on Jesus our brother and the power of your Spirit, who upheld him. Show us yourself, and your Son, in our growth in favor with you and others. In Jesus' name we pray. Amen.*

# Unexpected Joy

# 16. YOU WERE MADE
# FOR CHRISTMAS

*The kingdom of heaven is like treasure hidden
in a field, which a man found and covered up.
Then in his joy he goes and sells all that he has
and buys that field.*

*Matthew 13:44*

I find few things more tragic than being bored with Christmas. Its spirit and magic, that alluring sense of supernatural goodness, are not just for children but for the grown-ups too. *Especially* for the grown-ups. God forbid that we ever get used to Christmas.

When we find ourselves just going through the motions in these precious days leading up to the great feast, we do well to ask ourselves if the real treasure has been hidden from our eyes. Our world increasingly makes every effort it can—the more subtle ones typically being the most effective—to cover over the real essence of Christmas. So one way to refresh the heart is to ask, *Who is this Christ whose birth we mark?* In particular, *How do the Christmas accounts themselves lead us to look at Jesus?*

## CHRIST THE LORD

The great wonder of the first Christmas—worth announcing with an angelic host and telling everyone who would listen—finds its heart in this: "Unto you is born this day in the city of David a Savior, who is Christ *the Lord*" (Luke 2:11).

Not only was this the advent of the long-awaited Christ, the Messiah—the specially Anointed One of whom God's people had pined and about whom prophets opined—but this was "the Lord." God himself had come. Here, finally, after centuries of waiting, was the true Immanuel. Here was "God with us" (Matthew 1:23).

It was news too spectacular to say all at once. Day after day would pour forth speech in the life of this child. Act after act would reveal piece by piece that this human somehow shares the divine identity of Yahweh, "the Lord" of Israel and over all nations. Page after page in the Gospels, story after story, shows us progressively more that this one who is so manifestly man is also truly God.

This Word who "became flesh" (John 1:14) is one and the same Word who was in the beginning with God, and is God, and through whom all things were made (John 1:1-3). This was the great spectacle for those shepherds and magi, and it is the wonder we ourselves, who have lived our blessed lives knowing this truth, should aspire to taste again each Christmas.

But he is not just God with us. It gets better. He has come to rescue us.

## CHRIST THE SAVIOR

God is with us in this Christ, and it is no circus stunt for mere entertainment. This is no raw demonstration that the Creator can be a creature if he wants. Rather, this marvel is for us: for our rescue from sin and all its pervasive effects, entanglements, and ruin.

"Unto you is born this day … *a Savior*," heralds the angel (Luke 2:11). "You shall call his name Jesus," the messenger says to Joseph, "for he will save his people from their sins" (Matthew 1:21). Jesus (Hebrew *Yeshua*), means "Yahweh saves." This same God sent Moses as his instrument to save his people from Egypt. He sent Joshua, and the judges, and the kings and prophets as his instruments of rescue at points in the past. And now he himself comes, and he comes to save.

But there is more yet to be said. It gets even better.

## CHRIST THE TREASURE

God himself arrives not only to save us from sin and death but to rescue us for himself. Christ comes and will pay the ultimate price in suffering and death "that he might bring us to God" (1 Peter 3:18), and that risen he would be our exceeding joy (Psalm 43:4).

This is what the Puritan theologian Thomas Goodwin (1600-1680) had in mind when he said that there are "higher ends" than Christ being God-in-the-flesh and coming to save God's people. All the benefits achieved by his life and death "are all far inferior to the gift of his person unto us, and much more the glory of his person itself. His person is of infinite more worth than they all can be of" (quoted in Mark Jones, *A Christian's Pocket Guide to Jesus Christ*, p 3).

Jesus himself is the great joy that makes all the attendant joys of our salvation so great. The risen Christ is the treasure hidden in the field (Matthew 13:44). He is the pearl of great price (Matthew 13:45-46). He is not just God with us, here to save us, but he himself is our greatest joy, the preeminent treasure, who will satisfy our human souls forever as only the divine-human Christ can.

## CHRIST THE GLORY

But Christmas doesn't terminate on our enjoyments. The herald is joined by the heavenly host: "Glory to God in the highest, and on earth peace among those with whom he is pleased!" (Luke 2:14).

Some of us like to call this mindset "Christian Hedonism." The joy which Christ came to bring in his own person as the God-man is the joy that aligns with, and fulfills, the great purpose of all creation. Christmas brings the electricity of joy that runs along the grid of all reality. Not only does God satisfy the human soul, but he is most glorified in us when we are most satisfied in him. Our joy serves his glory. God's "chief end was not to bring Christ into the world for us," continues Goodwin, "but us for Christ ... and God contrived all things that do fall out, and even redemption itself, for the setting forth of Christ's glory."

This child of Christmas is more than Lord. He is even more than Savior. He is our great treasure, and in our eternal enjoyment of him is his glory and the end for which God created the world. Christmas is not finally about his birth for our salvation but our existence for his glory.

You were made for the great joy of Christmas.

*Father in heaven, we acknowledge that the great joy of Christmas is Christ himself, and we marvel that such joy in us is not icing on the cake, or some added extra, but the live concern of God Almighty. With all your heart and soul, you see to it that the souls of your people are satisfied in your Son, to the glory of his name. Exalt him in us this Christmas. Satisfy our thirsty souls in him: not just in his salvation but in your Son himself. We receive him as the great gift of Christmas and gladly declare that we were made for him. In his precious name we pray. Amen.*

# 17. LEARNING THE HABIT OF CHRISTMAS

*None of us lives to himself, and none of us dies to himself. For if we live, we live to the Lord, and if we die, we die to the Lord. So then, whether we live or whether we die, we are the Lord's.*

*Romans 14:7-8*

Over the years, during the Advent season, I have habitually reached for two prized possessions. One was a Beach Boys Christmas CD that I came into possession of sometime in the late 90s—a tradition which now has slowly faded away. The other item, which has served my soul much better, and continues to do so to this day, is Donald Macleod's book *The Person of Christ*. My annual Advent habit is to read up on Christology (the study of the nature and work of Jesus Christ). I try to branch out some each year, but it always includes at least a little rereading of Macleod.

## HABITS FOR CHRISTMAS

We are, by nature, creatures of habit. This is not the product of the fall but of God's good design. Good habits help us flourish by enlisting our subconscious to carry out repeated functions so that we can direct our limited bit of brain power elsewhere.

Of course, sin plays havoc with our habits too, but an important part of practical redemption and holiness, by the power of the gospel and God's Spirit, is the creation, over time, of new habits—daily habits of hearing God's voice in his word and having his ear in prayer and walking with him in glad obedience; and weekly habits of belonging to and gathering with his body in worship.

Habits, however, are not just daily and weekly but annual as well. God made seasons (Genesis 1:14). That's why I feel something deep down in those first days of spring, in the hottest days of summer, in the coziness of fall, and in the first snowfall of winter. And for Christians, we have long linked December 25 with the birth of our Savior, and anticipated one of our two highest feast days with these weeks of liturgical anticipation that we call "Advent." And now we're but a week out from Christmas Day, with our final week of waiting ahead of us.

## SEASON OF WAITING

As we've seen, one vital aspect of this season is often missed today: *Advent is a season of waiting.* Whereas Lent, as a season, encourages a kind of whole-life consecration in anticipating the marking of Jesus' final week—and especially his sacrificial death for us on Good Friday and his victorious resurrection for us on Easter Sunday—Advent's particular note is one of patient waiting.

Each year, in our month of waiting to mark the arrival of God himself in human flesh, we remember the people of God who waited for centuries—centuries!—for the coming of the promised Messiah to rescue them. They had God's promises: a "seed of the woman" who would crush the serpent's head (Genesis 3:15; Romans 16:20), a prophet like Moses (Deuteronomy 18:15, 18; Acts 3:22; 7:37), a priest who would eclipse the first-covenant order (Psalm 110:4; Hebrews 5:4-6; 7:11-17), and a son of King David and heir to his throne (Isaiah 9:7; Matthew 1:1; 22:42) who would be greater than David, as his lord (Psalm 110:1). For centuries, God's people waited.

Yet they "did not receive what was promised, since God had provided something better *for us*" (Hebrews 11:39-40). Now we live in the era of the Messiah. Christ has come as the climax of history and shown us the Father and his great design. It is good for us, though, to rehearse in Advent the *anticipation* of God's ancient people to renew our *appreciation* of what we now have in Christ.

For this reason, Advent is a season of minor chords, captured so well in the hymn "O Come, O Come, Emmanuel." As we wait, we replay the centuries of longing and yearning that preceded the coming of Christ, and in doing so, our joy in and gratitude for what we have in Christ deepens and becomes richer and sweeter. And we too live with longing and yearning—for Jesus' second coming—even as our waiting now takes on a fundamentally new shape, because of his first coming.

Then, on Christmas Day, those minor chords break into the bright, festive major chords of "Joy to the World," resolving the tension of ages past, even as they point us to the second coming for which we hope.

## THIS CHRISTMAS WILL CHANGE YOU

God's good and powerful gift of *habit* teaches us an important truth for the Advent season, and especially as Christmas Day now draws near: holidays and feasts not only fill our mouths with laughter, and our bellies with food, but shape our souls, for good or ill.

December is the single most distinctive month in our society, and Christmas the most distinctive day. It has its own special décor and music. It has the most distinguishing feel. Now Christmas lies only a week away, and we cannot miss it. Christmas confronts us and affects us. It makes us either more like Scrooge (from Charles Dickens' *A Christmas Carol*) or more like the shepherds who glorified and praised God (Luke 2:20). Come December 26, we will be different, to some degree, whether more like Herod or more like the magi who "rejoiced exceedingly with great joy" (Matthew 2:10).

This Christmas will change you. You will not be the same afterwards. You will be the better for it, or the worse. Will you be closer to Christ because of this Christmas, or further away? Will your heart be softer to him or more callous? Will more fog lie between your eyes and his face, or will you see him with greater clarity and savor him with greater fervor? Will you know and enjoy Jesus more?

## COME, LET US ADORE HIM

Let's not go through the motions. Perhaps today is the time to think afresh through your plans for Christmas Day, or to sit down with your spouse or a friend or family member to consider how to make the most of this Christmas Day for seeing and savoring the person of Christ. He is worthy of our best daily, weekly, and annual habits.

*Father in heaven, how marvelous that your people waited centuries, and yet here we are, in the age of the Messiah, conscious of your grace and your grand design to visit us in the person of your Son. Rekindle our awe in this final week before Christmas. The incarnation of your Son is truly awe-inspiring. Keep us from being steamrolled by secular assumptions and patterns. Inspire in us fresh initiatives and habits to remember what's at stake and who we celebrate in these precious days. In Jesus' name we pray. Amen.*

# 18. CHRISTMAS DOESN'T IGNORE YOUR PAIN

*[We are] sorrowful, yet always rejoicing.*

*2 Corinthians 6:10*

Some buoyant personalities can celebrate Christmas even in hard seasons of life, seemingly unfazed. But for others, all the talk of joy and merriment at Christmas can make our sorrows feel all the more acute and our pains all the more painful. Normal life is hard enough. It's even harder when all the world seems to be singing, ringing bells, and pretending everything's suddenly merry. The pressure to feel the joy of Christmas can make joy all the more difficult.

The real Christmas, however, does not ignore our pain. When we open the pages of Scripture and turn to that first Christmas, we find, without doubt, that all was not merry and bright. The new glimpses of merriness that do emerge fall against a backdrop of misery and disorder. Those first rays of brightness shone in a land of deep darkness.

## MARY AND JOSEPH

First, consider Mary. Doubtless much excitement and anticipation came with the angel's announcement—along with great confusion and misunderstanding. Soon she would be showing. She was betrothed but unmarried. Soon the watching eyes of her native Nazareth would make her the subject of their whispering and judgments. Even three decades later, her son's enemies would play the card when outmaneuvered: "*We* were not born of sexual immorality" (John 8:41, emphasis added). If Jesus couldn't leave such rumors behind, then even less could Mary.

And consider Joseph. His betrothed "was found to be with child" *before their marriage*. What disgrace would have attended this news for him? How deeply hurt must he have felt to find her pregnant? She had seemed so wonderful, so chaste, so favored by God. What dreams were certainly shattered? What turmoil he must have faced, for however long those hours and days dragged on between learning of her pregnancy and the angel later appearing to him in a dream, appealing to him to "take Mary as [his] wife, for that which is conceived in her is from the Holy Spirit" (Matthew 1:20). Joseph trusted the angel's words, but he must have had his momentary lapses. And word of his dream wouldn't have stopped the gossip around town.

## SINS HE CAME TO TAKE

More significant than Joseph's or Mary's pain, however, is the pain and sin and suffering and ruin for which

Jesus came. The angel declared to Joseph, "You shall call his name Jesus, for *he will save his people from their sins*" (Matthew 1:21, emphasis added). Every Jew agreed that God's people needed saving—from Roman occupation and dominion, that is. The coming of Christ was at least a reminder of their political subjugation to pagan Gentiles. But the angel's announcement to Joseph didn't even mention Rome. God's first-covenant people indeed needed saving—from their own sins: from the darkness and corruption within them.

If God's people, not to mention the nations, weren't needy—and desperately so—there would have been no Christmas. Christ did not come to put on a show or make a cameo appearance in history. He came to bring life to the dead, to rescue the perishing, to heal the sick, to destroy the works of the devil. For centuries, misery and darkness had been compounded. Only in coming to save such a depraved and disfigured world would his arrival signal hope for any real merriment and brightness.

## A SWORD TO PIERCE YOUR SOUL

Yet the relief of our pain would come through his. Mary must have experienced a shock when she presented her newborn son in the temple. An old man named Simeon declared his sense that this child was the Christ, but then he turned to look Mary in the eye and spoke to her a sobering prophetic word:

> *Behold, this child is appointed for the fall and rising of many in Israel, and for a sign that is*

> *opposed (and a sword will pierce through your*
> *own soul also), so that thoughts from many hearts*
> *may be revealed. (Luke 2:34-35)*

Her child being the Christ would not mean immunity from controversy, enemies, and great pain—but precisely the opposite. And Mary herself would have "a sword … pierce through [her] own soul also." What could this mean but that some great tragedy was appointed? Could her own soul be pierced by anything other than his premature death?

## JOY DEEPER THAN SORROW

The earthly life that began at Christmas was not to be an easy one: not at birth, not in infancy, not in adulthood. Isaiah had prophesied that the Christ would be despised and rejected, and he was; that he would be a man of sorrows and acquainted with grief, and indeed he was (Isaiah 53:3). But this life, painful and challenging as it would be, was not unacquainted with the deep, deep joy that could sustain the man of sorrows.

Christmas doesn't ignore our many pains; neither does it bid us wallow in them. Christmas takes them seriously—more seriously than any secular celebration can—and reminds us that our God has seen our pain and heard our cries for help (as in Exodus 2:23-25; 3:7-9; 6:5), and he himself has come to deliver us.

Christmas, at its best, gives us a peek of the uncompromised joy that is coming, and as we glimpse it, even from afar, we have a foretaste. Like the apostle Paul, and the man of sorrows himself, we are "sorrowful yet always rejoicing" (2 Corinthians 6:10). We may be overwhelmingly sorrowful at Christmas, and yet, in Christ, by his Spirit, God can give us the resilience to rejoice.

*Father in heaven, in our toughest seasons of life, it's good to know that you're not pressuring us to feign merriment. You see our pains. You hear our cries for help. And what greater demonstration of your care and concern could we have than that you sent your own Son into our world of sin and chaos and frustrations that first Christmas to come to our rescue? O Father, in our sufferings and stress, grant that we do not ignore the great display of your love in sending your Son to die for us. Touch our souls this Christmas. Show us that real joy is possible, even in the midst of pain. Give us a glimpse and foretaste of the glory to come. In Jesus' healing name we pray. Amen.*

# Our
# Unexpected
# Part

# 19. CHRISTMAS TESTS OUR TREASURE

*It is more blessed to give than to receive.*

*Acts 20:35*

'Tis the season to test our treasure. The days lead-ing up to Christmas bid us dig deeper in our wal-lets than any other season.

Which may be a great annoyance for Scrooge—but it is a great opportunity for the Christian to put to the test one of the great realities in the universe: "It is more blessed to give than to receive" (Acts 20:35). Consider three truths for Christmas spending and year-end giving.

## 1. MONEY IS A TOOL

It can be easy to forget that the problem isn't money but our hearts. It is not money, but "the love of money," that is "a root of all kinds of evils" (1 Timothy 6:10), and from which we should keep our lives free (Hebrews 13:5). Finances, salaries, and budgets themselves are an important part of the world that our Lord created and entered into as a creature.

When people asked him about taxes to Caesar, Jesus didn't decry the evils of money but relativized its value in relation to God (Matthew 22:21). When they came looking for his temple tax, he didn't rebuke them but made (miraculous) provision for both himself and Peter (Matthew 17:27). He even commended, in the face of Judas's objections, Mary's lavish display of love in anointing his feet with expensive ointment worth more than a year's wages (John 12:3-8). Jesus would have us go so far as to "make friends for yourselves by means of unrighteous wealth, so that when it fails they may receive you into the eternal dwellings" (Luke 16:9). In other words, money is a tool that can be used for long-term Godward goals, not just short-term selfish purposes.

And tools are made to be used. Holding on to money will not satisfy our souls or meet the needs of others. And Christmas is a good time to put our finances to work in the service of love.

## 2. HOW WE USE MONEY REVEALS OUR HEARTS

Matthew 6:21 holds an important reminder for every December: "Where your treasure is, there your heart will be also." Hoarding our money says something: that we fear not having sufficient resources for the future. Penny-pinching betrays our unbelief in the provision of our heavenly Father (Matthew 6:26) and his promise to "supply every need of yours according to his riches in glory in Christ Jesus" (Philippians 4:19).

Giving, on the other hand, is an opportunity to show, and reinforce, the place of faith and love in our hearts.

It's a chance to gladly cultivate the mind of Christ through our spending: "Let each of you look not only to his own interests, but also to the interests of others" (Philippians 2:4).

But the greatest test of our treasure is not *whether* we're willing to spend it, but *who and what* we spend it on. In particular, Christmas is an occasion to look past the small joys of self-oriented spending, and pursue the greater pleasures of spending on others.

## 3. SURPLUS AND SACRIFICE VARIES FROM PERSON TO PERSON

Hoarding and generosity aren't the only options. For most of us, the vast majority of our spending goes to meet our own everyday needs and those of our families. God provides us with income for such purposes. And to many of us, he gives resources beyond our needs and enables us to join him in the joy of giving to others.

This raises the question of what qualifies as "our needs." Is it simply food, clothing, and shelter in meager proportions? Where is the line between righteous and unrighteous spending on ourselves? The great bishop and theologian Augustine of Hippo (354-430) offers us one time-tested standard in "the needs of this life," summarized by author Rebecca DeYoung as being...

> ... *not just what is necessary for bare subsistence, but also what is necessary for living a life "becoming" or appropriate to human beings. The point is not to live on crusts of bread with bare*

> *walls and threadbare clothes. The point is that*
> *a fully human life is lived in a way free from*
> *being enslaved to our stuff. Our possessions are*
> *meant to serve our needs and our humanness,*
> *rather than our lives being centered around*
> *service to our possessions and our desires for them.*
> *(Glittering Vices, p 106)*

No doubt, discerning what is (and is not) "a fully human life ... free from being enslaved to our stuff" will vary from person to person, place to place, and age to age. "Each one must give *as he has decided in his heart*" (2 Corinthians 9:7). We do well to be more critical of ourselves than of others on this score, remembering how prone we are, when it comes to money, to be hard on others and easy on ourselves.

One reality to acknowledge is that "a fully human life" is not a static existence. God made us for rhythms and cadences, for feasting and fasting, for noise and crowds, and silence and solitude. So we are wise to avoid both extremes of sustained opulence and sustained austerity. And while discerning precisely what's too little or too much is no easy task, John Piper wisely observes, "The impossibility of drawing a line between night and day doesn't mean you can't know it's midnight."

One important test is *sacrifice*. Do you ever abstain from something you'd otherwise think of as "the needs of life" in order to give to others? Few acts lay bare our hearts like sacrifice. When we are willing not only to give from our excess but to embrace some personal loss for the sake of showing generosity toward others, we say loudly and clearly, even if only to our own souls, that we have a greater love than ourselves and our comforts.

## THE MOST CHEERFUL GIVER

In the end, as cheerfully as we may give, we cannot out-give the truly cheerful Giver. Willingly, he gave his own Son (John 3:16; Romans 8:32), as he had decided in his heart, not reluctantly or under compulsion but with overflowing joy.

God loves cheerful givers because he is one—the supreme one. And every gift we give in Christ is simply an echo of what we have already received and of the immeasurable riches to come (Ephesians 2:7).

*Father in heaven, here at Christmas save us from the heart of Scrooge, and make us more like you. You are truly the ultimate Giver. Christmas expresses your stunning generosity. You gave your own Son to the constraints and miseries of our humanity and world. And what love you have demonstrated in history, for all to see, in that while we were still sinners, Christ died for us. So, Father, bend our hearts to be more like yours this Christmas. May we know, as never before, the heights and depths and riches of the blessedness of giving. In Jesus' name we pray. Amen.*

# 20. WORDS ARE THE GREATEST GIFTS

*I have spoken to you, that my joy may be in you,*
*and that your joy may be full.*

*John 15:11*

**W**ords may be the best-kept secret of Christmas. Even more important than the items we purchase and the packages we wrap are the letters we write and the phrases we utter. And once you discover the secret, you might spend less time sweating over what to buy and give more energy to crafting what to say.

Jesus' own words are what should make us pause and ponder the power of words at Christmas, and all year long. In John 15:11, he says to his followers:

*I have spoken to you, that my joy may be in you,*
*and that your joy may be full.*

It's one thing to feel happy for a fleeting moment. It's quite another to have Jesus' own joy coursing inside of you—not only to *taste* joy but experience *fullness* of joy. So how does that happen? How does Jesus' own delight—dwelling in him, empowering him, filling his soul—become ours? How does his happiness come to dwell in and empower and fill us?

The answer, he says, is the wonder of *words*. Words are God's vessel for passing joy from one soul to another.

## JESUS' OWN JOY IN US

Our human lives are awash in words. We encounter (and produce) tens of thousands of them every day. We're prone to take their function and power for granted, when we should regularly marvel.

In John 17:13, Jesus turns to his Father and prays about his disciples:

> *Now I am coming to you, and these things I*
> *speak in the world, that they may have my joy*
> *fulfilled in themselves.*

All the things Jesus said (and then caused to be captured and preserved for us in the Gospels) he said not just that we would have joy, but that *his own joy* in his Father might be in us. It's almost too magnificent to contemplate. If Jesus himself had not said it, we would not presume it were so.

But Jesus really does mean to share *his own joy* with us. And he does so *through words*. He designs that his followers hear and receive his words, and feed their souls on them, as the prophet Jeremiah was fed by God's word, and tasted them as his joy and delight (Jeremiah 15:16).

How can we not exclaim with John Wesley, "Oh, give me that Book"?

And Jesus models for us how we can pass his joy on to others, at Christmas and year-round. As joy fills and expands in a soul, it rises to the level of expression. The vocal cords sound, the lips and teeth move, and the words pass through the air and into the open holes in the sides of our head called ears. Invisible words pass into the open receptacles and down into our souls, and one person's joy feeds another's. Not just from Jesus to us, but from others to us—and from us to others. All through words.

## "MAGIC" WORDS OF JOY

If we weren't so familiar with words, and were to learn about their power for the first time, it would sound like magic. *You mean someone with a full heart of priceless joy in God can exhale, sound and shape these invisible vessels of joy (which pass through the air, into my head, and down into my soul), and by faith give me real and lasting joy?* Yes, it is amazing.

And it gets even better. As we draw from a full tank of joy, to transmit through words our joy to fill another's tank, our own joy doesn't go down but up! "Praise not merely expresses but completes the enjoyment," the author C. S. Lewis once said.

When we stay quiet about what makes us happiest, we don't preserve our happiness. Hearts don't stay full by us keeping the lid on them. Our joy dwindles when we stay quiet. But when our joy inspires us to expend energy to express it in understandable words—which can be hard work—our joy actually ripens, deepens, expands, and "completes the enjoyment." Giving ourselves to the effort it takes to carefully *say it* (or write it) both sweetens our delight and makes it more contagious. Others can share in it when they hear about it.

Which makes us want to tell others not just *that* we're happy but *why*. What is the fuel on our fire? Instead of just saying, "I'm happy," why not say instead, "Messiah has come"? Instead of just saying, "I'm hopeful," say why you have hope. Instead of just saying, "Jesus is my treasure," say what specifically makes him feel supremely valuable.

## GOD'S OWN JOY IN HIS WORD

Perhaps we shouldn't be surprised that words hold such power—yes, for spreading discontent and ruining Christmas, but also for sharing joy and making it what it is.

After all, when God himself reaches into our world to communicate to us through his Son, he calls him "the Word" (John 1:1). God's Word in Jesus to us is so rich and deep and full and personal that what he sends forth is not just an invisible word but a Word-person. God has spoken to us, not just through prophets and apostles but "by his Son" (Hebrews 1:1-2). Jesus' person and work is the very embodiment and climactic expression of what God has to say to humanity—and the grace and joy he has to offer.

In his first advent, the Word became flesh that the very joy of God—eternal, unquenchable, unshakable—

might become our joy. That Word, his words, and our words about him are the greatest gifts of Christmas. So, let's learn the secret. Even more valuable than anything we can wrap in paper is the joy we can capture in words, whether spoken or written, to help fill others with the sweetest delight a soul can taste: Jesus' own fullness of joy.

*Father in heaven, this Christmas make our words your means of joy. Keep us from souring the great occasion of Christmas with the lingering discontent in our souls. Grant instead that the joy in us, through Christ, would rise to the level of sweet, encouraging, upbuilding, hopeful words. Make our mouths to be foundations of contagious joy in Christ this Christmas. May Jesus be honored in our words, and may the hearts of our friends and family be enriched, rather than encumbered, by the things we say. In Jesus' name we pray. Amen.*

# 21. LOVING HARD PEOPLE AT CHRISTMAS

*Have this mind among yourselves, which is yours*
*in Christ Jesus...*

*Philippians 2:5*

Most of our favorite Christmas songs are carols of joy, peace, and love in some form. Yet in reality, the busyness of the season—and the inevitable proximity to extended family—can make Christmas one of the most relationally challenging times of the year.

As we head into the relational trials and opportunities of Christmas Day, I'm reminding myself of three important texts that show how Christmas can *produce*, rather than *compromise*, love for others.

## LOOK TO THE INTERESTS OF OTHERS

The first Christmas began in the heart of God, or we might say, in the mind of Christ. When Paul tells Christians to "have *this mind* among yourselves, which is yours *in Christ Jesus*" (Philippians 2:5), what follows is the story of the incarnation, in sum, from heaven to earth: "[Being] in the form of God, [Jesus] did not count equality with God a thing to be grasped, but emptied himself, by taking the form of a servant, being born in the likeness of men" (Philippians 2:6-7).

What mindset gave rise to that first Christmas? Not the impulse to cling to private rights and privileges as God, but the willingness to inconvenience self and sacrifice comfort as man. Instead of grasping for privilege, Christ emptied himself of his rights. And Paul's corresponding charge to believers is just as appropriate during this season:

> *Let each of you look not only to his own interests,*
> *but also to the interests of others. (Philippians 2:4)*

The call of love begins with a call to look—to look to the interests of others. To get outside our own needs and preferences, to look beyond ourselves, and to see and seek to meet the needs and wants of others. How might it transform our Christmas gatherings if we were to genuinely "look ... to the interests of others," rather than be bent on recreating the perfect Christmas experiences from the movies or our memories?

## GLADLY SPEND AND BE SPENT

Having been freed from the prison of self to see the interests of others, what do we do? How do we go about meeting others' needs? Paul's insight into "love" in 2 Corinthians 12:15 is powerful, and particularly so at Christmas:

*I will most gladly spend and be spent for your
souls. If I love you more, am I to be loved less?*

Paul's fatherly care hadn't always *felt* loving to the Corinthian Christians. So here he implores them not to turn their hearts from him but to see that he really *does* love them. On what evidence? On the fact that he "will most gladly spend and be spent for [their] souls." Paul will embrace costly and inconvenient personal losses for the sake of their gain. In other words, he will give what is his—time, energy, attention, possessions, money, comfort, peace of mind—in order to benefit them. And he does not do it begrudgingly or dutifully but *gladly*—because, in the words of Jesus, "It is more blessed to give than to receive" (Acts 20:35).

## REMEMBER THE GREAT POSSESSION

But that is easier said than done. In our sin, we so easily default to selfishness and self-focus rather than looking to the interests of others. How do we keep loving, even when it's hard?

Hebrews 10:32-34 recalls a time when some in the early church were put in prison for their faith, and others, instead of going into hiding, went public to visit them in prison (out of love). In doing so, they exposed themselves to the same persecution. Their possessions were plundered by official decree or mob violence. How did they receive that?

Hebrews reminds them: "You *joyfully* accepted the plundering of your property" (Hebrews 10:34). Not only did they *accept* it, but they did so with *joy*. But how? Where did this come from: to *joyfully receive* such personal loss, to look to the interests of others, and to *gladly* spend and be spent? It was because…

> *You knew that you yourselves had a better*
> *possession and an abiding one. (Hebrews 10:34)*

The word for "property" is the same word, in the plural (*hyparxontōn*), as the word for "possession" (*hyparxin*). So, literally, "you joyfully accepted the plundering of your *possessions* because you knew you had a better and abiding *possession*."

Because these Christians had God as their heavenly treasure, they were able to accept the loss of their earthly treasures in the calling of love. And not just accept, but *joyfully accept*. They joyfully accepted the loss of their finite, earthly, limited plural possessions because *they knew* they had the infinite, heavenly, all-satisfying, singular possession, whose name is Jesus.

If such joy in their great possession could strengthen them to endure all that they suffered and lost, how much more might it inspire genuine love and generosity in us at Christmas? Not just giving our money and material possessions as gifts but also giving our more treasured possessions—our time, energy, comfort, convenience, and attention.

### THEY REMEMBERED
The *knowing* will make the difference when it comes to

the call of love—not just having the great possession, who is God himself, but *remembering* that we have him: "You *knew* that you yourselves had a better possession and an abiding one" (Hebrews 10:34).

Such *knowing* makes possible in us the true joy of Christmas, which is not selfish but self-sacrificial. It is "sacrificial joy." When we enjoy God and his Son as our great possession, we are finally free to surrender our small, private enjoyments for the greater enjoyment of meeting the needs of others and pointing them to our treasure.

The call to look to the interests of others, to gladly spend and be spent, and to remember our better and abiding possession is not a call to give up true Christmas joy but the opposite—to truly taste the depths of delight that God himself came to bring.

*Father, help us to forget self and embrace the greater joy that comes with self-sacrifice for the good of others. At Christmas, of all times, we need to remember that love "does not insist on its own way" (1 Corinthians 13:5). Fill us with satisfaction in your Son and your mercy, and make us instruments of your grace to others, especially those nearest to us who can be the hardest to love. In Jesus' name we pray. Amen.*

# That Unexpected Day

# 22. SWADDLING GOD

*This will be a sign for you: you will find a baby
wrapped in swaddling cloths and lying in a
manger.*

*Luke 2:12*

Luke is the only Gospel that mentions the swaddling
cloths, and it does so twice in just a few verses—
to ensure that it's not lost on us. Mary, we know, "gave
birth to her firstborn son and *wrapped him in swaddling
cloths* and laid him in a manger" (Luke 2:7). And it is
one of two details given by the angel later that night to
the shepherds, to help them find the child: "wrapped in
swaddling cloths and lying in a manger" (Luke 2:12).
Other than "born this day in the city of David" (Luke
2:11)—Bethlehem—this is all they had to go on: city,
swaddling cloths, manger.

It probably wasn't all that hard to find the child. The
main coordinate was Bethlehem, which wasn't a large city
but a nearby town, modestly sized. It wouldn't take long
to ask around and find out if anyone knew of a newborn.

The confirming detail would be that the baby would
be *lying in a manger*. That's distinctive. Indeed, Luke

reports this as the key detail confirming that the shepherds' search had ended: they "found Mary and Joseph, and the baby *lying in a manger*" (Luke 2:16).

Why, then, mention the swaddling cloths? Unlike the manger, it was not unique or distinctive at all. So far as we know, every newborn would have been swaddled.

First-century Jewish care for newborns was in step with the typical practice across the ages and around the world. Swaddling was "the normal practice of Jewish mothers," according to commentator Grant Osborne. "These are lengthy strips of cloth bound around the child to keep the limbs straight and still. The purpose was to keep them secure and provide stability" (*Luke Verse by Verse*, p 67). "The wrapping of his fragile limbs in cloths," confirms Darrell Bock, "was common in the ancient world to keep them protected and in place" (*Luke*, p 83).

## WHY SWADDLE?

The main point, then, of the angelic mention of this detail, and Luke's report of it, was *the commonness* of swaddling. Jesus was like any other baby. Swaddling was standard infant care. And Jesus was, in this way, a standard, very typical newborn in the care of loving parents.

His swaddling cloths are not a mark of poverty (for that, look to the two turtledoves sacrificed by his parents in Luke 2:24, according to the provision of Leviticus 12:8 for the poor). Rather they are a mark of the commonness of his newborn humanity. God himself embodied the same frailty and helplessness that every single one of us did at birth.

At long last, the long-awaited Christ has come—and he has come *like this*. *This* dependent on his mother and human father. *This* weak and vulnerable. *This* insecure and frail in the moments after leaving his mother's womb. "Fullness of God in helpless babe," as a hymn by Stuart Townend puts it, he cannot even control his limbs enough to keep himself asleep. He is this in need of warmth and protection. He is this in need of being settled and soothed. He is this human, fully human, beginning the journey of human life like the rest of us—from ovum to zygote to embryo to fetus to newborn—with all its attendant frailty and fragility. He is *this normal*: wrapped in swaddling cloths.

## HUMBLING ONLY BEGUN

Yet he is not normal. This newborn is *lying in a manger*. While the swaddling accents his commonness, the manger signals the extraordinary. This Christ-child is unexpectedly typical and surprisingly distinct. He is normal and yet not. He is fully human, and yet he is more than other humans. Set apart before the ages began, here he lies—on hay the animals will eat.

"The arrival of the incarnated Son of God," comments Bock, "is a study in contrast between how God did it and how we might have done it" (p 86). This indeed is the Christmas we didn't expect. From the virgin conception, to the parents of lowly estate, to the little town, the undignified visitors, and now the manger, God does it like no human would have planned.

And on top of it all, this child was born to die. He

"emptied himself"—not by subtraction of divinity but by addition of humanity—"by *taking* the form of a servant, being born in the likeness of men. And being found in human form, he humbled himself..." (Philippians 2:7-8). Already, lying in a manger, of all places, he was on the long, three-decades path to the cross. He abhorred not the virgin's womb, nor our flesh and blood, nor the place where animals feed, nor our world of suffering as he became "obedient to the point of death, even death on a cross" (Philippians 2:8).

## ONE LAST SWADDLE

Swaddled in the manger would not be the last time this human body would be bound. When they arrested him one day, he would be bound (John 18:12), and they would carry him bound from one unjust trial to the next (Matthew 27:2; Mark 15:1; John 18:24). Seemingly as helpless as a swaddled baby would be the man Christ Jesus, as he stood with chains on his hands and feet, and then was subject to a greater binding: with nails, to the cross.

The swaddling at his birth would not be the last time we hear of the incarnate Son being wrapped in cloth. After his death, he would be wrapped again, this time in linen—only to leave it behind when he walked out of the tomb alive. Among the synoptic Gospels (Matthew, Mark, Luke), only Luke (who mentions his swaddling) draws attention to the grave cloths: "Peter rose and ran to the tomb; stooping and looking in, he saw *the linen cloths* by themselves; and he went home marveling at what had happened" (Luke 24:12).

The infant in the manger would not stay swaddled. And his crucified body would not stay dead. He entered into the swaddled, bounded, frail, and fragile reality of our humanness, and carried us with him, even in our finitude, into the boundlessness of eternity and the coming new world. He is not dead; he is risen. The one who was, like us, swaddled is now the human king of the universe.

Still, it all began in such mildness and meekness. The one who would come from heaven to save us had to be truly us. The one who would pioneer our way into the very presence of God had to be like us in every respect, except sin. And so we marvel at both the normalcy of his swaddled humanity and the whisper of that unusual manger, in this singular child of Christmas.

*Father in heaven, what humility, what condescension your Son embraced to take our humanity! From the beginning, one humbling restriction after another formed and shaped his human life, as they do for ours. So, Father, here at Christmas, in remembering his infant binding, we also look to his adult binding at the cross, and we glory that he endured the chains and nails, and shed his grave cloths, for our sake. We are his, and he is ours. Draw us all the nearer to our Lord as we draw near the end of Advent and the arrival of Christmas Day. In Jesus' name we pray. Amen.*

# 23. THE REAL FESTIVUS MIRACLE

*Pray also for us, that God may open to us a door for the word, to declare the mystery of Christ ... that I may make it clear, which is how I ought to speak.*

*Colossians 4:3-4*

December 23 is circled on my calendar. It's marked as a day on which to take a deep breath, refocus, and head into Christmas Eve and Christmas Day with a fresh sense of what this often frenzied season is really about. In one sense, all of Advent is for this. But in another, it's nice to make a special effort on December 23 to recalibrate before Christmas Eve and Christmas Day.

By this stage, most of us are up to our necks in holiday craziness and commercialization. We may feel that we're once again stumbling toward Christmas exhausted and defeated by this most consumeristic season in our most consumeristic of societies. So it's time to grab the smelling salts, wake ourselves up from the trance of holiday hustle and bustle, and remind ourselves again, and our families, what we're doing anyways.

## SOMETHING FROM A SHOW ABOUT NOTHING

So how are we to resist the relentless commercializing of the Christmas season? We might be tempted to react like Frank Costanza, a memorable personality on the sitcom *Seinfeld*, who abandoned Christmas altogether and made up his own holiday, or anti-holiday, called "Festivus." In the 1997 episode "The Strike," Frank claims December 23 for this new observance, complete with an aluminum pole in place of a Christmas tree, an after-dinner "airing of grievances" among the family, and pranks that are dubbed as "Festivus miracles."

Frank's exasperation about what Christmas has become may resonate with you, not because you're the curmudgeon that he was but because you're an earnest Christian who would rather celebrate the unparalleled significance of Jesus' incarnation without all the frills and distraction of endless sales and endless Santa. But there is a better response to this seasonal malaise than abandoning Christmas altogether.

## THAT CURIOUS CHRISTMAS BLEND

Scottish theologian Donald Macleod shares some of Frank's frustrations but calls for a different solution:

> *Every year the world—and the church—experiences Christmas, that curious amalgam of paganism, commercialism, and Christianity which Western civilization has invented to tide it over the darkest days of the winter. Christmas is a lost opportunity, a time when the world invites the church to speak and*

*she blushes, smiles, and mutters a few banalities*
*with which the world is already perfectly familiar*
*from its own stock of clichés and nursery rhymes.*
*(From Glory to Golgotha, p 9)*

It's doubtful that the best way forward for Christians is to abandon Christmas and make up some new holiday that gets it all right. Macleod's solution has a better chance. When the world makes so much of a holiday once so deeply Christian, and thus tacitly invites Jesus' followers to speak, let's not blush, smile, and mutter a few banalities. Let's speak with clarity and conviction.

Let's talk in concrete terms about why we celebrate, and whom. Let's speak about the day when God became man, without ceasing to be God, that he might live among us as fully human and die the death we deserved.

Let's make it plain in our homes, and among our extended families, and for our friends, that Christmas is not just a sweet story for children but, as Macleod says, "the perforation of history by One from eternity … the intrusion and eruption of the Eternal into the existence of man." Christmas has a spectacular light that the seasonal glitz and glamor threatens to obscure, but it is much too precious to let it be dimmed.

The apostle Paul asks the Colossians to pray for his gospel ministry in a way that would be good for ourselves in the two days we have ahead: "Pray also for us, that God may open to us a door for the word, to declare the mystery of Christ, on account of which I am in prison—that I may make it clear, which is how I ought to speak" (Colossians 4:3-4). If Christmas is obscured everywhere, may it never be so in our homes and churches. May we make its real meaning clear—abundantly clear—which is how we ought to speak.

## THE FESTIVUS MIRACLE

Alongside that, we need to be vigilant to keep ourselves and those we love from being occupied with everything that has become Christmas, except the God-man in the manger. But for the Christian, the best answer to the Christmas mess isn't some new holiday. Our comeback is clarity about the true miracle of Christmas: that God himself, in the person of Jesus, took a true human body and a reasonable human soul (as the ancient creed puts it) so that, fully God and fully man, he might bring us humans from our mess to himself.

So perhaps this year the real "Festivus miracle" would be that a fictional anti-holiday would remind us here on December 23 to pause, catch our breath, and give some fresh effort to making central the true miracle of the God-man in our December 24 and 25 celebrations.

*Father, with Christmas now just two days away, renew our focus. May this Christmas not be a lost opportunity. As we gather with friends and family, help us to make the most of this occasion by commending and celebrating your Son. He is the great gift of Christmas. Thank you, Father, that you gave your own Son to dwell among us and die for us. And that you raised him. There would be no salvation, and no true comfort and joy, apart from your living Son. In his name we pray. Amen.*

# 24. THE DAY HEAVEN KISSED EARTH

*This is eternal life, that they know you, the only true God, and Jesus Christ whom you have sent.*

*John 17:3*

Christmas is the day heaven kissed earth.

This way of talking about the incarnation comes from the Puritan preacher and theologian Thomas Goodwin (1600-1680). He described the wonder of what happened at that first Christmas like this: "Heaven and earth met and kissed one another, namely, God and man" (*Works*, 4:439). The eternal Word—the golden Son of heaven—humbly and willingly took up our comparatively lowly humanity, without ceasing to be God, and entered into the created realm, coming to earth as one of us.

And it wasn't just for show. It was *for our sake*. The "great move" was all of grace and for our rescue. This begins history's climactic moment of love and favor. *Heaven kissed earth.*

## JESUS IS NO SUPERMAN

But don't misunderstand this great kiss. As we've seen, heaven's sweet kissing of earth in the incarnation didn't produce some mixture between the divine and human that was a third kind of being. Jesus is no superhuman—that is, not quite God but more than man. Rather, he is fully both—truly God and truly man.

Superman would be more palatable to both the theologically liberal and more conservative tastes. The liberal feels discomfort with Christ's full divinity, resistant to the idea that this Jesus might justly claim to have all authority in heaven and on earth, and rightly demand our allegiance, and spoil our perceived autonomy.

Meanwhile, the conservative is often uneasy with his full humanity. Something naïve in us prefers our Jesus to be sanitized: fully God but kept at arm's length from our earthiness. We quickly move past the weakness of the manger to Jesus as an adult, imagining a superman who breezed through life dispensing miracles at will, rather than a man of sorrows who struggled and suffered. But to do so is to underestimate the direness of our condition—about how bad things really are for us apart from Immanuel, about the extent to which he had to go to, and about the moral distance he had to travel to reach the muck of our planet and give us God's redeeming kiss.

Jesus is more than a baby in the manger, but he is nothing less. It's uncomfortable for sinners to face so squarely the gravity of our situation apart from heaven's rescue. But it's also deeply comforting for sinners who have recognized the decisive power of his salvation and given him their full embrace.

## CHRISTMAS FOR OUR BENEFIT

Christmas, then, is for our benefit. It's no birthday party for a tribal deity but the celebration of the King of the universe, who has come to save us. "You shall call his name Jesus," the angel says to Joseph, "for he will save his people from their sins" (Matthew 1:21). From its very beginning, the incarnation was about saving. Good Friday was always in view.

The meaning of Christmas is not just that he was *born among us*, but that he came to *die for us*. He came to secure for us eternal saving benefits. But there's more.

## WHAT'S BETTER THAN HIS BENEFITS

The "good news of great joy" (Luke 2:10) is more than just news of his birth and life. And it's more than just his death and what he obtains for us. The best news is *who* he obtains for us—himself and his Father. "This is eternal life," Jesus prayed on the eve of his crucifixion, "that they know you, the only true God, and Jesus Christ whom you have sent" (John 17:3). Which is as relevant at Christmas as it is any day.

Deeper than the Christmas narrative of his first coming, and the world-transforming Good Friday explanation about what his death accomplished, is this mindboggling truth: it's ultimately *we* who came into the world for *him*—for his glory—rather than he who came for us. In the decisive Christmas tally, it is not finally his arrival that makes much of us, but our creation and redemption that is designed to make much of him.

The Puritan Stephen Charnock (1628-1680) saw it similarly to his contemporary Goodwin. There is "something in Christ more excellent and comely than the office of a Savior; the greatness of his person is more excellent, than the salvation procured by his death."

The deepest significance of Christmas isn't just that Jesus came to save us, but that he is who he is. The great treasure isn't what the magi brought but the one held in Mary's arms. The surpassing value of Christmas isn't finally knowing ourselves to be saved but knowing the Jesus who saves us.

## MADE FOR THE GOD-MAN

The God-man in the Christmas manger—two full natures in one unique person—is, then, one focal point for our worship. Only in this one God-man do we find the truest "admirable conjunction of diverse excellencies." It is only this Jesus, who is both the Lion of Judah and the Lamb who was slain. He was a fragile incarnate infant in Bethlehem and is the triumphantly glorified almighty God at his Father's right hand. Only he is divinely *and humanly* tough and tender.

Because of this utterly unique union of God and man in one person, Jesus exhibits an unparalleled magnificence to those of us who are born again. No one can satisfy the complex longings of the human heart like the God-man.

Jesus is not just our substitute but our eternal satisfaction. He not only satisfies God's just wrath against us but satisfies the human soul forever. And because he is risen and reigning, we can enjoy him with unsurpassed delight forever. Heaven's kiss is the only one that will be eternally satisfying.

*Father in heaven, as the psalmist wrote, there is fullness of joy and pleasures evermore at your right hand—where now sits your Son. No one satisfies our soul like you, in the person of your Son. You made us for yourself. Give our souls rest this Christmas, and forever, in Jesus. In his name we pray. Amen.*

# THE PERMANENCE OF CHRISTMAS

*There is one God, and there is one mediator
between God and men, the man Christ Jesus.*

*1 Timothy 2:5*

Christmas is not only a chance to celebrate Jesus' *taking* of human flesh but also his *keeping* of it. It wasn't a mere thirty-something-year stint among us— impressive as that would have been. Jesus is forever the God-man.

To put it in the apostle John's language, the Word *became* flesh (John 1:14). His humanity isn't a costume. The eternal, divine Son didn't simply make a cameo appearance in the created world. He forever joined our humanity to his divinity and for all eternity will be fully God *and fully man*.

### "AS YOU SAW HIM GO"

We get a glimpse of this in Jesus' ascension, as Luke recounts it in the book of Acts:

> *As [the disciples] were looking on, [Jesus] was lifted up, and a cloud took him out of their sight. And while they were gazing into heaven as he went, behold, two men stood by them in white robes, and said, "Men of Galilee, why do you stand looking into heaven? This Jesus, who was taken up from you into heaven, will come in the same way as you saw him go into heaven." (Acts 1:9-11)*

He went up with a human body. He sits now in God's presence in his humanity. And he will return "in the same way as you saw him go into heaven"—in his humanity.

### KEEPING THE FORM OF A SERVANT

Philippians 2:5-8 speaks clearly about Jesus taking our likeness. But just as surely as he took it, so he also keeps it. In Philippians 3:20-21, Paul writes,

> *Our citizenship is in heaven, and from it we await a Savior, the Lord Jesus Christ, who will transform our lowly body to be like his glorious body, by the power that enables him even to subject all things to himself.*

Jesus didn't shed his human skin. He still has a body—a "glorious body," a perfected human body, a body like we haven't yet experienced but one day will experience when he transforms us.

Paul also makes reference to Jesus' continuing humanity in 1 Timothy 2:5:

> *There is one God, and there is one mediator*
> *between God and men, the man Christ Jesus.*

Here Paul, writing long after Jesus' ascension to heaven, is not afraid to refer to Jesus in the present as "the *man* Christ Jesus."

Jesus' work as the perfect mediator between God and man is not only dependent on his death in history at the cross but also on his continuing humanity. In his humanness, we are united to him by faith, and only in him are we united to God.

## THROUGHOUT HISTORY

Throughout church history, the best of Christian theology has recognized and affirmed the truth of Jesus' continuing incarnation—the idea that Jesus didn't simply play human for three decades in the created world, but rather forever joined our humanity to his divine person and will always be fully God *and fully man*.

In the second century, the apologist Justin Martyr was explicit in affirming that after the resurrection Jesus ascended in "the flesh in which he suffered" (*Fragments on the Resurrection*, ANF, Vol. 1, p 9). In the third century, the North African theologian Tertullian (about 160-225) wrote, "Jesus is still sitting there at the right hand of the Father, man, yet God ... flesh and blood, yet purer than ours" (*On the Resurrection of the Flesh*, ANF, Vol. 3, p 51). Some 200 years later Augustine spoke of "that one grand and health-giving miracle of Christ's ascension into heaven with the flesh in which he rose" (*The City of God*, NPNF, first series, Vol. 2, p 22.8).

Skip forward to the Reformation and we find the Scottish reformer John Knox writing in the *Scots Confession* that Jesus returned to heaven in "the self samyn body" (*The Works of John Knox*, Vol. 2, p 102). Then in the twentieth century, Swiss theologian Karl Barth wrote that Christ's humanity is "to all eternity ... a clothing which he does not put off. It is his temple which he does not leave. It is the form which he does not lose" (*Church Dogmatics, Vol. IV: The Doctrine of Reconciliation*, Part 2, p 100-101). (These quotes and more can be found in Gerrit Scott Dawson's good book *Jesus Ascended: The Meaning of Christ's Continuing Incarnation*.)

## FOREVER THE GOD-MAN

From the New Testament until the present, Christian theologians have rightly celebrated that Jesus is forever the God-man. He is glorious not merely in assuming our human nature but in remaining our brother and continuing as the visible "image of the invisible God" (Colossians 1:15).

Why does this matter? Without his continuing humanity, there would be no humanity in the Godhead to which we may be joined for all eternity. In *Jesus Ascended*, Gerrit Scott Dawson writes,

> *If [Jesus] dropped the hypostatic union with humanity, then he dropped us, and we are left forsaken on this side of the great divide, unable*

*to fulfill our purpose, find forgiveness and
restored communion, or enact our mission.*

But Jesus *hasn't* dropped us. Likewise, pastor and author
Douglas Wilson, writing with his typical flair, affirms
that when Jesus Christ became man…

> … *he was not "slumming" for thirty-three years,
> only to return afterwards to his old pre-incarnate
> state. He became a man in order to be our high
> priest—so that there would be a man praying
> for us at the right hand of the Father—and he
> continues to occupy this office, and will occupy it
> forever … Christ is our high priest continually
> (Hebrews 7:3). This means that the second person
> of the triune God became a man forever. God
> is clearly up to something that goes far beyond
> anything we might be able to imagine. But among
> other things, this means that if God has invested
> himself in this way in the future of the human
> race, it follows that the future of the human race
> must be stupefyingly glorious.*

Praise the divine Word that, without ceasing to be God, he
truly *became* man! He is forever fully God and fully man
in one person, now in the Father's presence, interceding
unshakably for those who are united to him by faith. Our
salvation is as sure as his continuing incarnation.

# SELECT BIBLIOGRAPHY

Tokunboh Adeyemo (ed), *Africa Bible Commentary* (Zondervan, 2010)

Gerrit Scott Dawson, *Jesus Ascended* (P&R, 2004)

Rebecca DeYoung, *Glittering Vices* (Brazos Press, 2009)

Wayne Grudem, *Systematic Theology* (IVP, 1994)

Mark Jones, *A Christian's Pocket Guide to Jesus Christ* (Christian Focus, 2002)

Donald Macleod, *From Glory to Golgotha* (Christian Focus, 2002)

Donald Macleod, *The Person of Christ* (IVP, 1998)

Grant Osborne, *Luke Verse by Verse* (Lexham Press, 2018)

David L. Turner, *Matthew*, Baker Exegetical Commentary on the New Testament (Baker, 2008)

N. T. Wright, *Who Was Jesus?* (Eerdmans, 1993)

# GENERAL INDEX

# SCRIPTURE INDEX

# ✳ desiringGod

Everyone wants to be happy. Our website was born and built for happiness. We want people everywhere to understand and embrace the truth that *God is most glorified in us when we are most satisfied in him.* We keep an archive of more than forty years of writing and sermons, as well as a daily stream of new written, audio, and video resources to help you find truth, purpose, and satisfaction that never end. If you want to learn more, we invite you to visit us at desiringGod.org.

desiringGod.org

---

## thegoodbook
### COMPANY
**BIBLICAL | RELEVANT | ACCESSIBLE**

At The Good Book Company, we are dedicated to helping Christians and local churches grow. We believe that God's growth process always starts with hearing clearly what he has said to us through his timeless word—the Bible.

thegoodbook.com | thegoodbook.co.uk
thegoodbook.com.au | thegoodbook.co.nz
thegoodbook.co.in